THE
MITFORD
GIRLS'
GUIDE
TO LIFE

THE MITFORD GIRLS' GUIDE TO LIFE

LYNDSY SPENCE

FOREWORD BY
JOSEPH DUMAS

The
History
Press

This book is dedicated to the following:

My family,
the Counter Hons, Lola & Harriet
and The Mitford Society.

And most especially Stephen Kennedy, a Honnish
friend in every way.

Illustrations by Tessa Simpson
Back cover image courtesy of the Mitford Archive

First published 2013

The History Press
The Mill, Brimscombe Port
Stroud, Gloucestershire, GL5 2QG
www.thehistorypress.co.uk

British Library Cataloguing in Publication Data.
A catalogue record for this book is available from the British Library.

ISBN 978 0 7524 9694 8

Typesetting and origination by The History Press
Printed in Great Britain

CONTENTS

Foreword

By Joseph Dumas

When Jessica Mitford died, in 1996, the British press opined that Great Britain in the twentieth century could be viewed through the prism of the Mitford family.

Jessica, whom I came to know in America and London in her final years, was the second youngest of the six Mitford sisters, daughters of the 2nd Baron Redesdale. On two occasions I met Pamela, the second-oldest sister, and on several occasions and through correspondence, Deborah, the Dowager Duchess of Devonshire, the youngest born and now only surviving sister.

By their own accounts, the Mitford girls, a sister act without parallel, were reared to sparkle.

If the Edwardian era – whose spirit haunted the Mitford household – was measured, say, in slow time, the arrival of the Roaring Twenties ushered in new concepts of motion: motor cars, air travel and all-night parties. By contrast to the silent and inflexible mores of the Edwardians, the Roaring Twenties materialised like a poltergeist unleashed.

Meanwhile, in their leafy, cloistered enclave in the Cotswolds, the sparkling Mitford sisters began to crackle. One could say Nancy – the eldest, who went on to write comic novels and highly regarded biographies – snuck in the gramophone, wound up its crank, positioned the trumpet, then took to the dance floor in fast time. Soon it became a sister act and none, ever, danced the 'Wallflower Waltz'. Their sparkle, which had begun to crackle, soon detonated.

As the author J.K. Rowling – a fan of Jessica Mitford's books – has noted, 'The story of the extraordinary Mitford sisters has never been told as well as they tell it themselves'. Keen observation, cracking humour and deft turns of the pen must have been encoded in the Mitford DNA. To them, we owe a debt of joyous gratitude; to their biographers and editors, including, amongst others, Diana's son Jonathan Guinness and his daughter Catherine Guinness, and especially Charlotte Mosley, Diana's daughter-in-law, we, the public, owe a debt of gratitude.

'The Mitford Industry' is the moniker the sisters themselves, tongue in cheek, appropriated about standing in the crosshairs of the media: scores of newspaper and magazine articles; books; radio programmes; television documentaries; plays; and even a musical. To this catalogue should be welcomed *The Mitford Girls' Guide to Life* by Lyndsy Spence. In today's techno-savvy world, with its iPads, iPhones and Android devices, Spence's breathless and delightful narrative could be seen as a 'Mitford app' for today's fast-paced reader.

Joseph Dumas, 2013

Acknowledgements

First and foremost I should like to thank my friend Stephen Kennedy for his encouragement, ideas, knowledge and original sources. Without Stephen's thoughtful guidance the book would not have taken a unique approach in telling the Mitford story.

I am also extremely grateful to the following people for their contributions: Goldie Newport for kindly sharing her invaluable memories of Pamela Mitford; Debbie Catling for her photographs, stories and suggestions; Fiona Guinness for providing me with private photographs from her family album; Jim Dixon, PDNPA, for sharing his personal photographs of the Dowager Duchess of Devonshire; Constancia 'Dinky' Romilly and Benjamin Treuhaft for their kind permission to use photographs of their mother; Andrew Budgell for his proof-reading and generosity with his time; Diana Birchall for her personal recollections of Jessica Mitford; Theo Morgan for his archived material; Leslie Brody for her patience in answering my emails and for sharing her contacts with me; David G. Lees, Sholom and Meems Ellenberg for sharing their personal photographs of Mitford residences; Locanda Cipriani for their personal photograph of Nancy Mitford; Tessa Simpson for her illustrations.

I am also grateful to the following people for their guidance and advice, and for providing material even though it may not have been produced in the printing of this book: Mark Beynon; Kimberly D. Davis; Matthew Doran; Colin Jones; Anne Morgan-Kendry; Karen Leonard; Michelle Morgan; Terence Towels Canote; Margot Smith; The Mitford Society.

I should like to extend a special thanks to Joseph Dumas for penning the foreword to this book and for his kind permission to reproduce unpublished material on Jessica Mitford.

Author's Note

The following books have been helpful in constructing this story: *A Fine Old Conflict* by Jessica Mitford; *A Life of Contrasts* by Diana Mosley; *A Talent to Annoy* edited by Charlotte Mosley; *Debs at War* by Anne de Courcy; *Decca: The Letters of Jessica Mitford* edited by Peter Y. Sussman; *Diana Mosley* by Anne de Courcy; *Diana Mosley, A Life* by Jan Dalley; *Hons and Rebels* by Jessica Mitford; *James Lees-Milne, Diaries: 1942–1954* edited by Michael Bloch; *Life in a Cold Climate* by Laura Thompson; *Love from Nancy* edited by Charlotte Mosley; *Loved Ones* by Diana Mosley; *Memories of Andrew Devonshire* by Deborah Devonshire; *Nancy Mitford* by Harold Acton; *Nancy Mitford* by Selina Hastings; *The Bookshop at 10 Curzon Street, Letters Between Nancy Mitford and Heywood Hill* edited by John Saumarez Smith; *The House of Mitford* by Jonathan and Catherine Guinness; *The Letters of Nancy Mitford and Evelyn Waugh* edited by Charlotte Mosley; *The Mitford Family Album* by Sophia Murphy; *The Mitford Girls* by Mary S. Lovell; *The Mitfords, Letters between Six Sisters* edited by Charlotte Mosley; *The Pursuit of Laughter* edited by Martin Rynja; *The Viceroy's Daughters* by Anne de Courcy; *The Water Beetle* by Nancy Mitford; *Wait for Me* by Deborah Devonshire.

Introduction

The Mitfords

How ghastly all the Mitfords sound, though of course in real life, ha-ha, they are ideal.

– Diana

Never have there been more talked about sisters than the six Mitford girls. They were the beautiful daughters of Lord and Lady Redesdale (known to their children as Farve and Muv), and were, in order of birth: Nancy, Pamela, Diana, Unity, Jessica and Deborah. There were sixteen years between Nancy, the eldest, and Deborah, the youngest. This large age gap divided the sisters into two different generations which, in a way, made them almost like a separate family.

Nancy, Pamela (to a limited extent) and Diana mixed with the Bright Young Things and experienced London's high society at the height of its glamour. They were young adults at a time when one could hop from foreign holiday to country manor on very little money, but of course it did help if one was part of the inner circle of the British aristocracy.

Unity, the quintessential middle child, wavered between childishly gushing to her elder sisters and throwing her weight around with the younger set; she was a stereotypical lost soul who went to dangerous lengths to find her niche away from her dazzling older sisters.

Jessica and Deborah were playmates and confidantes; separated from the older sisters, they relied on each other's company until Jessica eloped with their second cousin, Esmond Romilly. Deborah and Jessica experienced the 1920s and 1930s from the secluded security of the family home, Swinbrook House, with only their animals to keep them amused.

The girls were products of the autodidact method of learning and were renowned for their intelligence and quick wit; an extraordinary accomplishment when one remembers that they had no formal schooling at all. Nancy and Diana were quite ashamed of their lack of schooling and more than made up for this by educating themselves culturally through art, music and literature. 'Pity not to be educated, and it comes out more in writing than in speaking when one can slur things over a bit,' Nancy complained to Evelyn Waugh.

They were fluent in several languages, all except Deborah who never bothered to learn the customary French taught at home by their French governess, Zella. Unity, too, never learned to speak French as she felt it was an affected language, thus it never appealed to her.

Nancy could not spell in English or in French, and could not do arithmetic either. Diana, the most intelligent sister, resembled a formal schoolroom product with her perfect grammar, accurate spelling and vast knowledge of intellectual topics.

It was Nancy and Jessica's childhood ambition to go to school. They longed for a conventional education based on curriculum and structured learning, not to mention socialising with people other than their own siblings. They bitterly resented their mother's choice of home schooling. Unity briefly attended a day school but was quickly expelled for her nonconformist behaviour. Unity's habit of plucking her eyebrows was given as the excuse for her expulsion. Muv was quick to add, 'Not expelled, darling, asked to leave!'

The girls were relieved of their mediocre lessons by attending a children's dance class in the village. This recreational treat abruptly ended when one afternoon their instructor was running late and Jessica seized the opportunity to lead the children on to the roof to explain the mechanics of reproduction. 'And – even the King and Queen do it!' she eagerly told the little girls.

A few weeks later, Muv sent for Jessica. Following her scolding, Jessica learned that one little girl had 'awakened night after night' with screaming nightmares; she had grown pale and was on the verge of mental collapse when her governess had pried the truth from her. After that Jessica was shunned from children's parties and other juvenile social rituals which the neighbouring children attended and participated in. The story was not quickly forgotten, and a decade later during her debutante season, Jessica was still remembered as the bold girl who knew where babies came from. Quite a scandal in its day.

Friendships outside of the family were heavily discouraged by their parents. Muv worried if one of the girls received an invitation to a friend's house, 'Oh dear that means we have to invite them here!' Farve, however, had a simpler excuse; he disliked outsiders and people in general.

Until they were 18 and coming out as debutantes, the girls had only each other as company, 'Like a lost tribe, separated from its fellow men, gradually develops idiosyncrasies,' Jessica wrote in *Hons and Rebels*. They founded secret societies: The Hons Cupboard and the League against Nancy, spelled 'Leag' in their childish scrawl, and the linen cupboard served as their headquarters. Nancy set up her own troupe of Girl Guides as a tease towards Diana and Pamela, who loathed the idea of saluting her. And two private languages were invented: Honnish and Boudledidge.

In contrast to their contemporaries, the girls had an easy time at home. They were never forced to eat anything they disliked, they never had a strict routine and their parents never interfered in their daily lives around the house. As well, an extended trip abroad was part of the upbringing for each girl. In her teens, Nancy toured Florence with a group of friends, and, except for Unity and Deborah, they each spent six months in Paris as a sort of finishing school before coming out as debutantes.

The girls had very little supervision abroad and used this to their advantage. Unity chose to visit Munich where she lodged *en pension* with Baroness Laroche, and filled her days studying art and learning German. In Paris, Jessica quickly befriended a lecherous Frenchman who took her to a brothel. Her innocent eyes observed the many rooms, decorated to suit the clients' preferences, noting that one room served as a moving carriage, equipped with clever suspension to shake the room. Deborah travelled around Austria and Italy with her friends, an experience which she described in the code name of 'Angela Brazil' – the author who penned popular risqué novels about upper-class schoolgirls.

Muv whisked the three youngest girls away on 'cultural cruises' of the Adriatic and Mediterranean. And in winter the entire family visited Switzerland, where Deborah, a talented ice skater, had been scouted for the British Junior Team. Thinking that she would miss out on her childhood if she were a child sports protégée, Muv denied Deborah the opportunity. Deborah, at the time, was disappointed.

Private languages, inappropriate love affairs and sibling rivalry bonded the sisters together. All six girls led very distinct, cultural lives and not one sister, except for Diana and Unity, shared the same opinion or ideology. Also, each had their own maddening set of personality traits which both charmed and infuriated those who knew them, and those who read about their antics in the society columns.

Despite being penny poor in comparison to many of their aristocratic contemporaries, the girls' station in life and their birthright as Honourables (children of a lord) afforded them certain privileges that were out of reach to the working classes. But with little money, no formal schooling and a rather unconventional childhood, it is extraordinary when one looks at their ability and the resourcefulness they had to have to survive the many obstacles which appeared in their lives.

The girls absorbed every cultural detail around them. They were self-taught, well travelled and fiercely independent. These characteristics have been both vilified and celebrated their legacy; few said no to the girls, but would they have listened if they had? Of course not. The girls decided what they wanted to be at an early age, and they set about achieving their goals during their lifetime. They each possessed a strong sense of destiny and accomplished so much on so very little. Fascinating, don't you think?

—◠◡◠—

❧ NANCY MITFORD ❧

'French Lady Writer'
1904–73

I can't help seeing my childhood (and the whole of my life) as a hilarious joke.

– Nancy

Nancy was the ultimate tease, feared by her younger siblings and treated with suspicion by just about anyone who moved in her exclusive circle. She associated with the Bright Young Things, and despite being the daughter of a lord, she had to survive on a shoestring allowance. Instead of paying bills and buying necessities, Nancy spent her money on taxis and parties, and after a short spell of living independently in London, she returned to the family home, complaining that her floor was overflowing with clothing simply because she had no one to pick up after her: 'Oh darling, but you should have seen it. After about a week, it was knee-deep in underclothes. I literally had to wade through them. No one to put them away.'

After her brief social hiatus, Nancy's craving for excitement brought her back to the bright lights of London. She returned to the capital and accepted a job at her maternal grandfather's publication, *The Lady* magazine, where she wrote placid articles for genteel ladies, and in between she freelanced for *Vogue*. Nancy wrote her first novel, *Highland Fling*, which was a minor success upon its release in 1931. This meant that she had a respectable cheque to spend, but true to form, she squandered it, was broke again and peddling out chatty articles for a modest payment.

Although by far the wittiest sister, it would be a while before Nancy triumphed as a best-selling author. Before finding her niche, she would waste time wallowing in her own self-inflicted misery and falling in love with unsuitable men. 'Money and writing are curiously divorced from each other in my mind. The money always feels like having won a lottery when it comes.', Nancy said.

In 1928, Nancy met Hamish St Clair-Erskine, the flamboyant second son of the Earl of Rosslyn. Hamish possessed the most 'enchanting looks', though was not 'strictly handsome', and to those who knew him he was openly homosexual. But that did not prevent Nancy from falling in love with him, and according to Deborah, she was quite naive and unaware of his sexuality. Both were emotionally immature and behaved 'like a couple of twelve year olds'. Nancy and Hamish became engaged, and she invented a romance between the two, though the highlight of their evenings consisted of them dressing up in chiffon and putting vine leaves in their hair. Sometimes Nancy would curl Hamish's hair with her curling tongs and, in her opinion, 'He looked more than lovely'.

Her brother, Tom, tried to warn her off 'gay as gay' Hamish, for he had conducted a brief affair with him at Eton, but this did not deter Nancy as it was not unusual for men of that generation to experiment with homosexuality. Jessica said of the times: 'Some stuck to it, some didn't, but nobody paid much attention either way.'

Hamish had a fondness for heavy drinking and he frequented sleazy nightclubs. Nancy tolerated his strange behaviour, and this façade of a romance lasted for five years during a critical phase of her life. Time was running out for her to find a suitable husband; she was approaching 30, humiliated by her situation and desperate to fix it.

Nancy had a serious admirer in the form of Sir Hugh Smiley, a suitor which any debutante mother could only ever hope for. He was an aristocrat, rich and owned a 'gingerbread' mansion. Sir Hugh proposed marriage several times, and although tempted by his offer, Nancy could not bring herself to accept, for she was all too aware of the confinement of an influential marriage. Around the same time, she had cordial relationships with three other men, but Hamish's amusing qualities drew her back to him.

The allure of Hamish helped Nancy to avoid the complexities of an adult relationship which, at the time, she had many conflicting emotions about. Nancy wrote a letter to Tom, expressing her preference to earn a living as a writer so she could avoid marriage; it was, as she said, her desire to be financially and spiritually independent. In the same letter, she immediately contradicted herself and added that marriage and children were high on her agenda. She would accomplish neither so long as Hamish was in her life.

The charade finally ended in 1933, when Hamish could no longer carry on with the prospect of marrying Nancy and he feigned an engagement to another aristocratic woman. After Hamish's abandonment, and faced with the cruel realisation that she had ruined her chances with decent men, Nancy to considered suicide.

At the age of 29, and going nowhere romantically, Nancy fell into a rut and married the first man who asked her. Nancy's love interest was an irresponsible, heavy-drinking, notorious philanderer from an aristocratic family named Peter Rodd. Nancy promptly nicknamed him 'Prod'.

An intoxicated Peter, as a joke, had asked Nancy to marry him at a house party. To his surprise Nancy accepted. Before Peter could rectify his phony proposal, Nancy had announced their nuptials and set about arranging a hasty wedding. Although Peter tried to back out of their engagement, he could relate to Nancy for he was also at a loose end and his family was pressuring him to marry. This seemed to be the only thing they had in common.

After their marriage in 1933, life continued on as normal. Peter pursued his aimless existence of gambling and philandering, and Nancy complained of never having any money. Nancy was aware of her new husband's infidelity but she did not chastise him; she had only married him because she had hoped, in vain, that marriage would provide her with financial security.

Nancy chose the wrong husband for what she had in mind; Peter was the second son of Lord Rennell and, as such, would never inherit his father's title or his wealth. He received a small allowance, but when compared with the materialistic gifts bestowed upon his elder brother, this token seemed inadequate. Nancy and Peter's allowances from their families were scarcely enough to cover the rent of Rose Cottage, their modest house by the river in Chiswick, a West London suburb. To earn money, Nancy resumed her writing career and Peter drifted from job to job.

Nancy suffered two miscarriages, and as the months turned into years, she was forced to acknowledge the cruel reality that her marriage was in name only: 'I thought of writing down the bald facts of my life, not for publication but as a record. But they are so very odd I wonder if people would believe.'

In 1939, Peter enlisted in the Welsh Guards and Nancy thought he looked glamorous in his army uniform with 'masses of gold on his hat and a wonderful coat lined with scarlet satin'. However, during his absence, Nancy began an affair with a Free French officer, Colonel André Roy, a few months later she suffered an ectopic pregnancy. Her in-laws suspected the child was not Peter's, but this did not stop Nancy from complaining that they had snubbed her during her lengthy stay in hospital: 'My mother-in-law was told by the surgeon I should be in danger for three days and not one of them even rang up to enquire let alone sending a bloom or anything. I long to know if they bothered to look under *R* in the deaths column.'

Nancy recovered, and her affair with the tuberculosis-stricken André Roy came to an end. During this time Nancy accepted a job at Heywood Hill, the charming bookshop in Mayfair. She also fell in love with another Free French officer, Colonel Gaston Palewski, who would change the course of her life forever.

In 1945, Nancy became a best-selling author with *The Pursuit of Love*, and she relocated to newly liberated Paris. Nancy arrived in Paris and promptly telephoned Gaston. 'Oh how marvelous, how long are you here for, the weekend?' he enthusiastically enquired. 'No,' she answered, 'forever.'

Reflecting on her childless state, Nancy said:

> *I mind less and less not having any (children) except I do think when they are puppies, from 1 to 4 they are rather heaven. 4 to 20 is unbearable.*

From 1942, until her death in 1973, Nancy carried on a hopeless one-sided affair with Gaston, whom she nicknamed 'The Colonel'. He inspired her writing, encouraged her love of France and eventually broke her heart, when in 1969, after decades of stringing Nancy along, he married one of his many rich mistresses, Violette de Talleyrand-Périgord, the Duchesse de Sagan.

In 1969, Nancy became ill with cancer but her sisters kept the fatal diagnosis from her. Believing that she was getting better, Nancy began to pen her autobiography, which she had planned to call, *One*, but died before its completion. Nancy's swansong ended with a rather dramatic turn of events, perhaps best suited to her romantic novels. Gaston was driving past her Versailles house one afternoon when, suddenly, he felt the urge to visit her. Gaston turned the car around and raced back to find Nancy on her deathbed, and always the gentleman, his presence confirmed to Nancy that he had, in fact, loved her, and this provided some comfort before she died.

'Do you think everybody's real life is quite different from what they manage to make it seem?' she once asked.

❧ PAMELA MITFORD ❧

'Woman'
1907–94

Oddly enough I feel just as I did before I was eighty – somehow I had expected some magical change to take place but all is as usual.

– Pamela

Pamela was born three days before Nancy's third birthday, an event which hurled Nancy into a 'permanent rage'. The two sisters were complete opposites in looks and in temperament: Nancy was dark haired with triangular green eyes whereas Pamela had fair hair and large blue eyes. And unlike her elder sister, Pamela was a docile child whose later stereotypical female virtues of housekeeping and cooking would earn her the nickname, 'Woman'.

To the public, Pamela was also known as the 'Quiet Mitford' because her name had remained out of the headlines, unlike her five sisters who were tabloid darlings whether they courted the press or not. Pamela did not care for the superficial trappings of the London social scene and her earliest ambition in life was to be a horse. Pamela suffered from shyness and possessed a gentle nature; however, she more than made up for this with her adventurous spirit.

When her sisters were indulging in scandalous pastimes, Pamela could be found single-handedly motoring around Europe in her grey Morris Minor which she nicknamed 'The Stork', accompanying Farve on his gold-prospecting trips to Canada, managing Biddesden Farm, flying across the Atlantic (she was one of the first commercial passengers to do so) and, in her later years, contemplating writing a cookbook.

Although quite solitary in comparison to her lively sisters, Pamela was not without her admirers. Clever men fell in love with her and her most famous suitor, John Betjeman, swooned 'Gentle Pam' in his unpublished poem 'The Mitford Girls'. He proposed twice and twice she rejected him. Pamela was briefly engaged to Oliver 'Togo' Watney, a country neighbour and heir of the leading brewing business in London which produced Watney's Red Barrel beer. The engagement was called off by mutual consent.

In her late twenties, Pamela fell in love and married the eccentric millionaire scientist Derek Jackson, whose volatile nature meant that life with him was never dull. Derek detested children and when Pamela discovered she was expecting their baby, he loaded her into the car for a trip along the bumpy Norwegian roads to purposely induce a miscarriage. His stunt worked. In Derek's opinion, the child would have been the wrong sex, a female, or the wrong colour, dark like him.

After the war, Pamela and Derek moved to Ireland where they lived as tax exiles. After fifteen years of marriage, they divorced in 1951. Pamela never remarried and spent much of her life motoring around the Continent with her dogs and lifelong companion, an Italian-Swiss horsewoman, Giuditta Tommasi.

❧ DIANA MITFORD ❧

'Honks'
1910–2003

Why is it that anything we say or do is always supposed to be so interesting? I wonder.

– Diana

Diana was the family beauty, 'with a capital B', and indeed one of the most celebrated beauties of 1930s high society. In her teenage years, Diana was described by her brother's friend, James Lees-Milne, as 'The most divine adolescent', and he compared her to Botticelli's seaborne Venus. James Lees-Milne also taught Diana to read the literary greats – Shelley, Byron, Keats and Coleridge – and fell so deeply in love with the 14-year-old that, in his later years, no woman could evoke such feelings from him. The fixation was one-sided on his behalf, and he decided that she was not the girl for him. They were to remain lifelong friends.

Diana was also pursued by her third cousin, Randolph Churchill, and several members of Nancy's inner circle were besotted with her. This did little to discourage Nancy's uncontrollable jealousy of her younger sister.

In 1926, Diana received an invitation to stay at Chartwell House, the Churchill's family estate in Kent. Diana and her Churchill cousins were encouraged to participate in the adult conversation and were invited to listen in on drawing room debates. On that particular visit, at the age of 16, Diana keenly observed the divided opinions on the General Strike and the plight of the miners. It was the first time she had been exposed to the forefront of political conversation, and it would later serve as the pivotal moment for igniting her interest in politics. After much consideration, she concluded that her sympathies lay with the miners.

That same year, Diana was sent to Paris for twelve months as a substitute for finishing school. She studied art at the Cours Fénelon, where she attended lectures given by visiting professors from the Sorbonne.

During her stay in Paris, Diana befriended her mother's old friend, the artist Paul César Helleu, who at the age of 65 became obsessed with the perfect proportions of her face. He sketched her several times, and despite their vast age gap, he fell in love with her. When Helleu died in 1927, Diana mournfully announced, 'Nobody again will ever admire me as much as Helleu did.'

Paris served as a learning curve for Diana, who experienced independence there for the first time and discovered that she enjoyed a cosmopolitan life away from the bleak atmosphere of the countryside and constant supervision of her parents and governess. She had foolishly written in her diary about an unchaperoned trip to the cinema with a young man, and when Muv discovered the diary, the questionable trip to the cinema cost Diana her freedom. This further provoked her longing to escape the family home.

People rather realised that I liked clever people. Painters and composers are more fun than businessmen.

In 1929, five months before her nineteenth birthday, Diana married the Hon. Bryan Guinness, an heir to the Irish brewing fortune and son of Walter Guinness, who a few years later would become the first Lord Moyne. Her reason for marriage was very straightforward: escapism. Diana longed to escape the dreary boredom of Swinbrook, and marriage to a wealthy young man was her only hope. By the time Diana was 21, she had produced two sons, Jonathan and Desmond. And in 1932, she met her future second husband, Sir Oswald Mosley, the leader of the British Union of Fascists.

Diana was content with being Sir Oswald's devoted mistress while he remained married to his long-suffering wife, Cimmie. Diana was not demanding nor did she expect Sir Oswald to leave his family for her; instead she had one simple request: he may remain devoted to Cimmie, but he must never cheat on her.

Diana and Bryan separated and she moved into a stylish townhouse in Eaton Square, just around the corner from Sir Oswald's flat on Ebury Street. The rent was paid for out of her generous allowance from Bryan, and she brought with her a small staff consisting of a maid, nanny, cook and butler. That same year, in 1932, her divorce from Bryan was finalised.

I did not mean to imply that I consider myself aristocratic, I certainly do not.

Cimmie, who had just given birth to her third child, developed acute appendicitis when the appendix burst and she was operated on. Thee evening before Cimmie had taken ill, Sir Oswald orchestrated an enormous row with her and left for Diana's house. Upon his return, he found her sitting up in bed after the operation, looking healthy and apparently on the mend. However three days later, Cimmie developed peritonitis and was dangerously ill. Diana realised the grave consequences which might follow should Cimmie succumb to the illness.

Cimmie's untimely death at the age of 34, in theory, left Sir Oswald free to marry Diana. He received opposition from family and friends who also believed Diana had been the cause of Cimmie's death. Vivien Mosley certainly blamed Diana for her mother's death: 'Peritonitis is what killed her but with Diana there, she didn't want to live.'

Sir Oswald was involved in several affairs at the time, including Cimmie's stepmother, Grace Curzon, and her sister, Baba Metcalfe, and decided to cool relations with Diana until things had settled down. Sir Oswald and Baba embarked on a motoring holiday across France with his three children, Nicky, Vivien and Michael.

During this hiatus from Sir Oswald, Diana accompanied Unity on a trip to Munich where they attended the Nazi Parteitag in Nuremberg. Their first impression of seeing Adolf Hitler addressing the crowds would change the course of Unity's life forever; although, in hindsight, Diana said of the event, 'We heard the speeches Hitler made, most of them very short, and we understood not a single word.'

In 1936, Diana and Sir Oswald were married, but marriage did not tame his wandering eye. She accepted his shortcomings and, with a degree of reflection, added, 'With sex, opportunity is so important'.

After her involvement with Sir Oswald and her friendship with Hitler, almost overnight Diana turned from the most celebrated young woman in London society to the most notorious. She was the only Mitford sister to be imprisoned, spending three and a half years in Holloway Prison under Regulation 18B (imprisonment without trial). Her private and public reputation never recovered and she spent the rest of her life living in France. She died in Paris at the age of 93.

—⁄∿∿⊱—

❧ UNITY MITFORD ☙

'Boud'
1914–48

I know I have a part to play and I can't bear acting it!

– Unity

Unity was by far the most notorious Mitford girl and was on par with Diana for gaining scandalous headlines during the 1930s and 1940s. Unity was prone to extreme behaviour and shocked her contemporaries when she took up with the British Union of Fascists. Unity went to great lengths to provoke a reaction from people: she gave impromptu pro-fascist speeches at Speakers' Corner in Hyde Park; Nazi saluted townsfolk in Oxfordshire; and wrote pro-fascist letters to mainstream newspapers. Her earliest letters from Germany, shocking in their anti-Semitic tone, were laughed off as a nursery-style prank. Nobody at the time took Unity's behaviour seriously.

Unity was a curious child who possessed an exceptional artistic talent. She would go off to the corner of the children's drawing room and create unique pieces of art: sketches, paintings and odd collages of fur and other materials. At the age of 8, she created an 'unforgettable' nude picture of a man walking through a field wearing a turban. Around his middle was a bag, out of which he scattered seed. The title of the picture was 'Abraham and his Seed Forever'.

Unity grew from an eccentric child into a moody teenager; she became obsessed with fascism and during a spell of boredom she took off for Munich to learn German and to study art. But her main reason to stay in Munich was very clear: to stalk her idol, Hitler.

Unity's antics in pre-war Germany shocked Britain, and on the day war was declared, she retrieved a pearl-handled pistol from her handbag and shot herself in the head. Unity survived the clumsy suicide attempt but it left her permanently brain damaged. She returned to England, all expenses paid by Hitler, and devoted her attention towards organised religion.

Years later, the bullet wound in Unity's skull became infected and she died in 1948. For many people, this prolonged suffering was deemed as poetic justice. People understood very little of Unity's nature when she was alive; even her closest family and friends have struggled to convey what made her so likeable and special. History has not remembered her kindly, and she will be forever condemned as the ruthless, anti-Semitic girl who loved Hitler.

—◊◊◊—

❧ JESSICA MITFORD ❧

'Decca'
1917–96

Invisible boundaries kept me boxed in from the real life of other people going on all around.

– Jessica

A summary of Jessica's life could simply read as: at 13 she was a devoted pacifist; at 15 she converted to communism; at 19 she ran off to the Spanish Civil War; and at 22 she found herself in America, an avowed liberal and passionate supporter of civil rights.

It was Jessica's greatest ambition to escape the repressive confines of the aristocracy. She loathed the trappings of wealth and privilege that her upper-class status was associated with, and in her early teens she took an interest in civil rights, which later developed into an interest for protecting the rights of those victimised by racism in America. As a joke to annoy Unity, Jessica declared herself a communist. The two opposing sisters would draw a line in the centre of the children's drawing room and stand on either side, hurling political books and records at one another, screaming obscenities as they fought to defend their political party. Something which started off as a childish joke quickly developed into a deadly serious ideology.

> I had made no real friends, had learned nothing, was no further advanced in planning my life. I cursed myself for not having the brains or ability to find my own way out of the deadly boredom that was enveloping me like a thick fog, out of the trivial, dull daily round of activities in which I found myself.

In 1937, after years of following Esmond Romilly in the press, Jessica finally met him during a weekend stay at their mutual cousin's country house and she was immediately infatuated with the rebellious public schoolboy. Esmond was recovering from a bout of dysentery, caught when he was serving with the International Brigades defending Madrid during the Spanish Civil War. To her delight, Esmond was impressed with her communist beliefs and utter disdain towards their aristocratic upbringing, and the pair devised a plan to run away. Esmond would be returning to Spain, working as a reporter covering the conflict for the *News Chronicle*, and, of course, he would be more than happy for Jessica to accompany him.

Jessica successfully tricked her parents with a forged invitation to join some friends on the Continent. Muv and Farve escorted Jessica to the station and ensured she was settled on the train. They were unaware that Esmond was waiting in a separate carriage, his face hidden behind a newspaper. As the train pulled out of the station, he and Jessica looked forward to their new life of joining the Spanish Civil War in the fight against fascism.

Eventually, Jessica's plan was exposed and her parents summoned her back to Swinbrook – an order which she ignored. Peter Rodd came up with the idea that, since she was under 21, it would be best to make her a ward of the court. This further repelled Jessica and Esmond, who viewed their loved ones as conspirators against their happiness.

Muv visited Jessica with the intention of bringing her home to England. Jessica thwarted any plans of returning home without Esmond when she confided to her mother that she was pregnant and, therefore, she *must* marry Esmond. To avoid another family scandal, her parents relented, and Jessica and Esmond were hastily married at the British Embassy with Esmond's mother and Muv as their only guests. Farve never spoke to Jessica again.

On their return to England, Esmond and Jessica set up home in a flat in Rotherhithe Street, East London, where their daughter, Julia, was born. Six months later their happiness was shattered when Julia succumbed to measles. Following the death of Julia, Esmond and Jessica, 'like people battered into semi consciousness', fled to Corsica and remained there for three months, 'returning only when the nightmare had begun to fade'.

In 1939 war with Germany was fast approaching and young men of Esmond's age would soon be called up. Esmond decided that they should move to America until the war had begun. They were enthralled with America, and in the wake of tragedy they hoped to start a prosperous new life. War was declared, and the outcome would change Jessica's life forever.

In 1941, Esmond's plane went missing over the North Sea. At the age of 24, Jessica found herself widowed and with a baby, Constancia 'Dinky' Romilly, to care for. In 1943, Jessica married Bob Treuhaft, a civil rights lawyer who held the same socialist views as her. Together they joined a communist party in California, fought for civil rights, and in the early 1960s they started the groundwork in exposing the fraudulent American funeral industry.

Following the success of her first book, *Hons and Rebels*, in 1960, Jessica became a full-time author and was often a guest speaker at American universities under the lofty title of Professor Jessica Mitford. Not a bad achievement for somebody who bemoaned the fact she had never been to school.

❧ DEBORAH MITFORD ❧

'Debo'
1920–

I freely admit that I long for __all__ sisters __all__ the time.

— Deborah

Lacking the restless ambition of her older sisters, and without a rebellious nature, Deborah revelled in tending to her hens, picking the fleas off her pet dachshund and partaking in the Saturday hunt. She also learned to drive a car at the age of 9. Despite her easy-going ways, Deborah had one eccentric quirk: an unhealthy phobia of school.

Much to her horror, Deborah had been sent to St Margaret's Bushey, a boarding school in Hertfordshire. She found geometry to be so incomprehensible that it induced her to faint, and the hot blackberry and apple pie and custard had made her sick. So after three days of hell, Muv removed Deborah because she feared an onset of pining. 'The headmistress kissed me goodbye! Beastly old lesbian', was Deborah's final farewell to conventional education.

At the age of 18, Deborah decided to 'live for pleasure'. But she could not forget her philistine ways and declined a trip to Paris because learning French would have interfered with a season's hunting.

In 1941, at the age of 21, Deborah married Lord Andrew Cavendish, the second son of the tenth Duke of Devonshire, who would become his father's heir after his older brother, William, was killed in 1944. In 1950, at the age of 30, she became the eleventh Duchess of Devonshire when Andrew inherited the title.

Deborah settled into a life of public duty and served as the chairwoman of many British organisations, including Tarmac. Her business acumen can be credited for the decision in opening Chatsworth (home to the Dukes of Devonshire) to the public and, in doing so, saved a family dynasty from succumbing to mountains of debt generated by the tenth duke's death duties.

In 1955 the family moved into Chatsworth and Deborah thought it best to undertake the mammoth task of overseeing the renovation; she personally chose the decor for the 175 rooms, 24 bathrooms, 21 kitchens, 3,426ft of passages, 400 windows and 17 staircases. Nancy was one of the first visitors to Chatsworth, and was so impressed by Deborah's skill and eye for detail that she remarked, 'Nobody else could have done it as well'.

In a similar light to her older sisters, Deborah was also prone to idol worship, which happened to be in the form of Elvis Presley, but sadly Deborah's crush developed later in life and she only fell in love with Elvis fifteen years after his death. If she had admired him during his lifetime, she claimed she would have been charged for stalking. It seemed the Mitford girls were not without their obsessions.

Nancy teased Deborah that she had the mental age of a 9-year-old, and often addressed her letters as: 'To Nine, The

Duchess of Devonshire.' Deborah disliked books and thought reading was a waste of her valuable time. Ironically, Deborah wrote several successful books and has gained quite a fan base in the literary world. Out of them all, Nancy claimed that Deborah was the natural writer in the family, and thank goodness she put that into practice.

———

THE PARENTS: 'MUV & FARVE'

My parents have been described as eccentric, although I did not consider them so, perhaps because it is impossible to imagine one's parents being any different than they are.

– Jessica

David Mitford (1878–1958), otherwise known by his formal title of Lord Redesdale, was always addressed as 'Farve' by his six daughters. Farve served as the inspiration for Nancy's much-loved character Uncle Matthew in her best-selling novels, *The Pursuit of Love* and *Love in a Cold Climate*. Farve lived a simple life, always happiest around his animals, and he found chatting to his country neighbours to be much more satisfying than mingling with smart society.

When in London, Farve frequented the Army & Navy Stores, and often sat in on debates in the House of Lords. Diana claimed that Farve was obsessed with sanitation and would have made a marvelous plumber; one of the reasons he objected to women joining the House of Lords was that he could not bear the thought of them using the lavatories.

He was a devoted philistine and had little time for modern extravagances. By the time Deborah was born, Farve had much mellowed, and the youngest Mitford girl, who shared his love of the outdoors, became his favourite child. Jessica summarised his temperament in her memoirs, *A Fine Old Conflict*: 'Farve was a man of violent passions and prejudices, the terror of housemaids and governesses – and of us children.'

Farve was a typical second son, considered to be of little use to his father. He was therefore not sent to Eton, like his elder brother Clement, but to Radley, a second-class boarding school. Upon leaving school, Farve ventured to Ceylon (now Sri Lanka) to sample colonial life during the golden age of the British Empire, where he decided to try his hand at tea planting.

The tea-planting venture lasted for four years and was not to be Farve's vocation in life, and he joined the Royal Northumberland Fusiliers when the Boer War broke out in 1898. Farve learned his favourite insult while in Ceylon: *sua*, which translates in to 'pig'. The infamous insult would live on in Mitford lore and find a new lease of life in Nancy's novels.

During his army days, Farve was wounded three times and in 1902 he suffered a chest wound which put him in a field hospital for four days. After his recovery, he was hauled back to camp in a bullock wagon. The children relished the tale for years to come, particularly the 'writhing nest of maggots' which had festered in his lung. From his hospital bed, Farve dictated a love letter to Sydney Bowles. Two years later, after he was invalided home from Africa, they were married.

I am normal, my wife is normal but each of my daughters is more foolish than the last.

– Farve

Sydney Mitford (1880–1963), whose formal title was Lady Redesdale, was referred to as 'Muv' by all of her children, and 'Granny Muv' by her grandchildren. She, too, has been immortalised in *The Pursuit of Love* and *Love in a Cold Climate* through the characterisation of Aunt Sadie. Muv was accused by her children of being vacant to the point of neglect, and on the day of Deborah's birth she vaguely scribbled in her accounts book, 'Chimney swept'. Muv had wanted six boys and one girl; instead she had six girls and one boy. Their parlour maid announced at the time of Deborah's birth, 'I knew it was a girl by the look on his Lordship's face!'

Muv had an erratic upbringing as one of four children, raised by her widowed father Tap Gibson Bowles. Tap sent his two sons to school but kept Muv and her younger sister, Dorothy, with him. Muv wore a sailor suit until the age of 18 and spent her childhood sailing on her father's boats, *Nereid* and *Hoylen*, taking year-long trips to the Middle East and frequent voyages to France.

When Tap returned to his London townhouse in Lowndes Square, Muv served as his housekeeper. Her dealings with the drunk, disobedient male servants encouraged a dislike for male staff and, as a strict rule, she only hired female staff to work in her own houses.

In the early 1940s, Muv and Farve separated but never divorced. Political and family differences, mainly Unity's pathetic existence after her suicide attempt and Muv's sympathies towards Hitler, tore them apart. Farve departed for Redesdale Cottage with their London housekeeper, Margaret Wright, and together they lived in a state of domestic bliss. Muv became Unity's caregiver and spent her remaining years on Inch Kenneth, her private Scottish island off the west coast of Mull.

When your parents were young, they were so beautiful they were like Gods walking upon earth.

– Farve's cousin to Diana

1

Keeping Up Appearances

An Index of Everyday Obstacles

Nancy is a very curious character.

– Muv

The Mitfords had a unique way of approaching everyday obstacles, often with the view that there was a funny side to everything. You too can use their approach, following their attitudes to such obstacles:

Adultery: Discretion and acceptance are everything.
Alcohol: Indulge in the occasional tipple, refrain from excessive drinking.
Alimony: Always accept.
Apologising: Sometimes a necessity in life but refrain from admitting blame.
Beauty: One is born with it.
Boundaries: Non-existent.
Bourgeoisie: Laughable.
Charm: According to Diana, charm was much more important than beauty.

Children: Deborah advised that one should love one's children but there is no rule in liking them.

Church: To relieve the boredom of the Sunday sermons, the children would lick the pews.

Coming Out: A seasonal trudge around the marriage market.

Corrective Surgery: i.e. Diana's car crash in 1935. Yes.

Cosmetic Surgery: Diana claimed that vanity prevented her from having a facelift.

Crime: A fascinating subject.

Day School: Prison to Pamela, Diana and Deborah. Freedom for Nancy, Unity and Jessica.

Death: A fact of life.

Disagreements: An argument is a great way to show off one's intellect.

Divorce: Be prepared for social suicide.

Exercise: Only if one has to wear tennis whites, a golf jersey or equestrian clothing.

Fancifier: How awful, Deborah thought, that two honest people like Muv and Farve could give life to such 'fancifiers' as Nancy and Jessica. A fancifier is a lovely name for a liar.

Friendship: In the style of Deborah, always refer to your female friends as 'the wife'.

Funerals: Sing *Holy, Holy, Holy* followed by absolute floods.

Holidays: To be spent on the Venice Lido.

Honourables: 'To be drowned at birth?' Discuss.

Illnesses: Denial can be comforting but not a cure.

Insults: Do make them memorable or forever hold your peace.

Jealously: It is rather a privilege to consume other people's thoughts.

Jobs: To be tolerated until one discovers their niche or something better comes along.

Language Barrier: Nod in agreement, and in the style of Deborah exclaim, '*Quelle Surprise!*'

Life: Seems to be, as Nancy claimed, a massive joke.

Love: A fleeting fancy.

Marriage: Essential if one is trained in little else.

Medication: Gleefully consume the forbidden fruits of one's childhood. See Muv's Medicines (p. 197).

Money: It was Nancy's motto that lack of money should never prevent one from having a good time.

Nicknames: A must, the more far-fetched the better.

Nightclubs: In the words of Diana, they are 'very dull-awful noise, second-rate jazz, hideous people, and lights going on and off'.

Nouvelle Rich: Terribly Non-U.

Organisations: It is in true Mitford fashion to get completely caught up in one's beliefs and whims.

Peer Pressure: What peer pressure? The Mitfords set the trend.

Politics: Causing family feuds since 1932.

Public Transport: Yes. In her youth, if Nancy had nothing to do on a Friday night, she would have hopped on board a double-decker bus for a trip through the leafy London suburbs.

Post Office: One is always at their mercy.

Religion: 'The Church of England', Diana freely admitted was, 'the fount of all evil'.

Shopping: As Nancy advised, shopping is an art form that takes years to perfect and cannot be accomplished in a weekend. One must carefully select and build a collection of clothing.

Swearing: Terribly Non-U.

Tanning: Nancy believed that a tanned complexion was nothing more than 'one mass of well-oiled cracks'.

Telephone: Farve only used the telephone if it was an emergency.

Travelling: 'All tourists half expect to be murdered,' Nancy once said, so it is awfully brave to attempt to travel. Do admit.

Unity [Mitford]: Testing one's patience since 1914.

Visitors: A terrible inconvenience. In the style of Farve, if one should be inconvenienced by house guests, one should bellow from the table, 'Have these people no homes of their own to go to?'

Weddings: See Nancy's Guide to Planning a Wedding (p. 152).

—*∿*—

How to Behave: Mitford Style

Maintaining a Persona: 'The Shop Front'

I may seem calm but everything is churning underneath.

— Pamela

As a rule, the Mitfords never allowed the outside world to catch a glimpse of how they truly felt about a certain situation. They hid their feelings, mainly sorrow, beneath an exterior known as 'The Shop Front'. This established persona was, as Nancy often told friends, founded in the nursery. The shop front, their chosen expression for trying times, took on many disguises. Nancy and Diana used humour to mask their heartache, whereas Pamela exuded calmness to the point of being vacant. And, despite her passionate views on things, and being very vocal about almost everything, Jessica, too, could blank out her true feelings to protect herself whenever she felt vulnerable.

She (Nancy) and Decca were (and are) equally economical with truth or whatever the expression for malicious imaginings.

— Deborah

When Nancy's marriage was failing, she would often invent funny stories about her husband and sail through life with an air of hilarity, taking nothing seriously, but behind the scenes she was deeply depressed and at a loose end. Nancy received the news of her brother's death while staying with friends, and rather than retreating to her bedroom under a cloud of grief, Nancy applied her make-up, changed into evening clothes and attended supper. She made a conscious effort to be bright and amusing all through the meal because she did not wish to spoil it for the other guests. Critics might dismiss this as being unfeeling or too afraid to face the facts, but friends often remarked on Nancy's bravery in desolate situations.

For the public, Nancy is the delightful writer of funny books. Nobody who hadn't seen Nancy could ever realise how vile Nancy could be.

– Deborah

Nancy's persevering nature paid off when she was visiting friends in Oxford. During the visit, she began to feel unwell and realised it was serious. Unsure of what to say, as she did not wish to make a scene, Nancy tactfully made up a story of having an attack of appendicitis. She carried her suitcase herself, so as not to show how ill she felt, and boarded a bus straight for London. Upon reaching London, she immediately checked into hospital. It turned out that Nancy was dangerously ill, suffering from an ectopic pregnancy, and to save her life she had to have emergency surgery, which banished all hopes of her having the children she desperately wanted. Rather than wallowing in the gloominess of her new situation, she put on a brave face. That was her way of dealing with things. The shop front *must* be maintained at all times.

The private Decca is Decca, but the public Decca is somebody unforgivably callous and hard.

– Diana

DOUBLE STANDARDS

It should not come as a surprise that each Mitford girl made up their own rules for living – and then changed them accordingly to adapt to whatever mindset they were in or whatever obstacle they faced. As we know, Jessica despised Diana due to her association with fascism, so it would seem natural that she would also loathe Unity for her close friendship with Hitler; after all, it was verging on the same principle. This is, in fact, wrong. Jessica adjusted her views to make room for her beloved 'Boud'. She blamed Diana for Unity's extreme beliefs, and for her early death in 1948. In Jessica's eyes, Diana was to blame for everything.

It would be three decades before the opposing sisters would meet again, briefly reuniting over Nancy's deathbed, and then going their separate ways until Jessica's death in 1996.

'The more I see of Bryan the more it surprises me that Diana should be in love with him, but I think he's amazingly nice,' Nancy wrote to their brother, Tom. 'Nice' was the preferable term used for describing Bryan. Indeed, he had a *nice* personality, a *nice* demeanour and a *nice*, gentle way of handling people; his nature was without malice and, unlike his sisters-in-law, he did not thrive on catty gossip or teasing people for his own amusement. But his niceness did not discourage Diana's wicked treatment of him.

Nancy was not the only person astonished to discover Bryan and Diana's unusual love match. Nancy predicted that Diana would soon grow tired of sentimental Bryan. Diana craved excitement and culture, whereas Bryan preferred to stay at home. As a pastime, Bryan wrote poetry: many poems were dedicated to Diana, but she cared little for his devotion. Here were two people, so different in spirit and in their awareness. He was blinded by love and admiration for her, so in essence, whenever she was conducting her affair with Sir Oswald Mosley she was knowingly wounding him each time. But it did not matter; his passive attitude seemed to endure her cruel treatment.

Even though Diana instigated her divorce from Bryan, she felt it best to blatantly remain in the family home, thus creating an uncomfortable atmosphere so Bryan would be forced to leave her. In doing so, Diana predicted, 'The onus was on him'.

Diana viewed Nancy as her only ally during the divorce proceedings from Bryan in 1932. For a short time, Nancy displayed an unshakable loyalty towards Diana, and moved into her spare bedroom at 'The Eatonary', the silly nickname the younger girls had given her posh townhouse in Eaton Square.

Muv and Farve disapproved of Nancy's siding with Diana, and they blamed her for encouraging Diana's decision to leave Bryan. Although she appeared to be completely loyal to Diana in her hour of need, Nancy was not above accepting a gift from Bryan when he sent her an expensive dress of white tulle for her wedding to Peter Rodd in 1933.

The gesture of buying Nancy a wedding present serves as an example of Bryan's personality. He wished to remain close to the Mitford family; he enjoyed the sibling camaraderie, the banter and teasing, and often holidayed with the family, minus Diana, during their annual skating holiday to Switzerland.

Although Diana devastated Bryan by leaving him for Sir Oswald, he was still besotted with her and found it difficult to evoke feelings of hatred. When she suffered broken facial bones as a result of a car accident in 1934, he rushed to her aid and arranged for the top plastic surgeon, Sir Harold Gillies, to tend to her. The previous doctor who tended to Diana had stitched her face together using rough thread due to the surgical thread being locked up for the evening. Had Bryan not intervened, her face would have been left badly disfigured. Upon her recovery, Diana left her sickbed and rushed to Naples to holiday with Sir Oswald.

Upon reaching Naples, Diana discovered Baba Metcalfe sunbathing on the terrace. She rushed into the villa to locate Sir Oswald, but he was at the beach with his children. He hurried up the steps to the villa to be confronted by his two mistresses. Diana, enraged by his deception, caused a scene. Wires had been crossed and Sir Oswald had not been expecting her until the following week. He had hoped to spend one week with Baba and the other with Diana, without either woman knowing about it. The exasperated Italian butler was overheard saying, 'It ees Mrs Guinness', when the children became alarmed by the raised voices. The next morning, Sir Oswald and Baba left for Capri. This disregard for Diana's feelings did little to discourage her relationship with him.

Family dynamics were firmly established in the nursery. Pamela stood alone, much more drawn to Muv than to her sisters, although in their later years she became the star of the family and her common sense was valued by all the sisters, especially Nancy whom she nursed through cancer and Diana with whom she travelled after Sir Oswald's death. Deborah claimed that Pamela still told her what to do long after she had grown up.

Jessica and Deborah were close in their childhood, and after Unity's departure to Germany, they grew even closer and shared a bedroom, always. It pained Deborah when she learned of Jessica's elopement with Esmond Romilly; how could she have deceived her, Deborah wondered. It was, as Deborah said, almost like a death in the family. Deborah could never forgive Jessica for tearing the family apart, disappearing without a trace and then cutting all familial ties once her secret was revealed.

Jessica and Nancy were most alike in their talents and in their wit. They had the same sharp tongue and eye for mockery, and got along wonderfully in person. But Nancy could not control her disloyalty to Jessica, and Jessica did not seem to mind much – she half expected it – and was disappointed when Charlotte Mosley withheld certain 'offensive' letters from Nancy's volume of letters, *Love from Nancy*.

The girls were alarmingly double-faced in their letters, about each other and to each other. Nancy 'dies for' Jessica and yet ridicules her behind her back. It was a common art practised by each girl in their endless correspondence, spanning decades; all except Diana. Yes, on the surface Diana was loyal to the core, not only towards her irrational beliefs but to her sisters too. Also, despite her association with Hitler and Sir Oswald, two figures of hate, she was very much 'the favourite sister'. Deborah adored her, which is obvious in her letters and recollections of Diana, and Diana loved her little sister. For almost a decade they were the only two sisters left: they could only write to each other and this confirmed their closeness. Deborah was present when Diana died during the notorious Parisian heat wave of 2003. 'I still pick up a pen to write to Diana,' Deborah solemnly said in an interview in 2010.

So, how could Diana win such admiration from her sisters, all except Jessica, of course? Nancy's teases tested the girls' nerves and Farve's rages put them on edge. Their mother was of little use in terms of companionship and Unity and Jessica were too busy with their political causes, something that was viewed as a lark. Pamela was vague and uninterested in them, and Nancy was 'a remote star'. Diana was reliable; her unchanging nature was a comfort to the girls and she was outwardly maternal to Jessica and Deborah. She taught Jessica to ride and gently prompted her, 'Do try to hang on this time, darling. You know how cross Muv will be if you break your arm again.' In their youth, Jessica adored Diana, Deborah claimed to hardly know her until she was much more grown up and Nancy came to rely on her generosity. Those attributes painted a saintly portrait of Diana, which in turbulent times the sisters still remembered. Diana's loyalty stood for something in the Mitford household, especially to sentimental Deborah.

DELUSIONS OF GRANDEUR

Nancy became an Honourable at the age of 12, 'by the skin of her pointed teeth', when Farve's eldest brother, the heir of the Redesdale estate, died in the First World War. However, it is a theory widely accepted by Nancy and explained in her infamous essay, 'The English Aristocracy', that the non-eldest children of a lord, especially girls, are in fact commoners as they cannot inherit their father's title or land, something which the entire monetary estate is tied to.

On that note, the Mitford message seemed to be that 'common' people should always behave as though one were an Honourable; good breeding often goes hand in hand with good manners. The Mitfords never changed their behaviour for anyone because it was their own natural character. Manners were instilled in the nursery and thus became a way of life. It has been said that, as a rule, when one is overly aware of one's own personality traits one becomes self-conscious of them. The Mitfords were never self-conscious about anything, at least not on the surface. Muv used the term 'what-a-set' when she was at a loss of words to describe anybody who behaved flamboyantly. It is a tactful description that contains a multitude of interpretations.

In 1967, a formal occasion hosted by Deborah brought Pamela into the company of Lord Mountbatten, who was the ambitious uncle of Prince Philip, great-grandson of Queen Victoria and previous Viceroy of India. Everybody had heard of him, and he and his glamorous wife, Lady Edwina, were prominent members of high society. 'I know you are Woman,' he mischievously said to Pamela. Pamela turned and barked, '*Yes*, and may I ask who you are?' Relaying the outburst, Nancy gravely wrote to Jessica, 'Collapse of stout party'.

Bryan would try to forget he was rich in a bid to be ordinary, when, in fact, Diana wanted to be anything but ordinary. Perhaps this is a good example of how new money and old money perceived things to be: Bryan's family had made their money from trade, whereas Diana was the daughter of a lord and her grandparents, on both sides, were in the peerage long before the Guinness family.

This façade caused problems in their marriage, and the pivotal moment in this ordinariness charade came when Bryan invited his architect friend, George Kennedy, and his wife to supper. Bryan thought it would make a good impression if he allowed the servants to have the night off and he optimistically suggested that they should cook the supper. Of course, Diana could see the insensitivity of the scenario. 'What that meant, of course, is that Poor Mrs. Kennedy, who cooked every night of her life, simply had to set to and peel potatoes yet again – Bryan couldn't do it. They weren't well off. What she would have liked was to have been taken to the Ritz.'

What a bore to be anything other than yourself, do admit.

LIFE'S LITTLE HURDLES

When Decca makes up her mind, she never changes it.

– Bob Treuhaft on Jessica

The key to getting through life's little hurdles is to make the best of a bad situation. For example, at first if one doesn't succeed, try, try, try again! Diana certainly adopted this approach when it came to getting what she wanted: a house of one's own at Holloway Prison. Determined to be reunited with Sir Oswald, Diana wrote to the government asking for permission to reside with him in prison. After several rejections, Diana was granted her wish and she and Sir Oswald lived in a parcels house in the grounds of Holloway, where they enjoyed the perk of having convicted bigamists as their own personal servants.

Of course, prison was a horrible experience for Diana. Rather than pleasing her critics by admitting the truth of the hardships she had suffered, in true Mitford form, Diana teased a newspaper reporter when she exclaimed, 'Going to prison turned out to be quite a surprise!' Diana's unpretentiousness and humour made her very popular in prison, and the prison guards who patrolled her wing claimed, 'We've not had such laughs since Lady Mosley was released'.

Make a Joke out of every Plausible Situation

Very ordinary, like a farmer in a brown suit.
— Pamela on Hitler

A strict governess had forbidden the children to use the expression 'damn'. And in true Mitford fashion, they invented a clever way around this by saying 'Amster*dam*' and 'Rotter*dam*'. The shock factor was just as good and the governess realised she was fighting a losing battle by forbidding the children to do anything.

Unity had little patience for their governesses and, always much larger than most adults in an age where the average height of a woman was just above 5ft, she would pick up their short governesses and place her on the sideboard. Needless to say, the children went through a series of governesses. 'Some were hopeless; some were brilliant,' Deborah said.

In the summer of 1929, Diana and Bryan sponsored a 'newly discovered artist' by the name of Bruno Hat. The poet Brian Howard and the artist John Banting produced a series of works on cork bathmats, framed with rope. An artistic interpretation that was very advanced for its day. The author Evelyn Waugh penned the foreword in the catalogue, 'An Approach to Hat'. The art exhibition was widely advertised and 200 guests were invited, including newspaper critics, for an exclusive audience with the self-taught artist.

Bruno Hat in appearance was an elderly German man confined to a wheelchair and disguised behind a bundled up scarf and an unruly beard. He spoke no English and muttered in unintelligible gibberish to the press.

Unsuspecting guests admired the strange artwork, praising the avant-garde approach, and Diana's great friend, the writer Lytton Strachey, purchased a picture to please Diana. The exhibition had been a great success.

The next day's newspapers were full of praise for Bruno Hat's artistic approach. Eventually the secret was revealed that Bruno Hat was the girls' brother, Tom, and the exhibition had been an elaborate hoax. 'Very dishonest,' Muv scolded Diana, but despite Muv's criticism, the Bruno Hat prank is remembered to this day, and in 2009 one of the pictures sold at auction for £18,000. 'I wish we had kept an outhouse full of them,' Deborah said.

When Diana's marriage to Bryan was on the rocks, she joked to Nancy that she planned to stock up on a trousseau of expensive clothes while she still had access to the Guinness fortune. She also remarked, 'I ought to get you a diamond necklace – last chance!'

The build-up to the divorce proceedings was becoming more and more sordid, with Bryan ready to accept liability.

In order to protect Diana's name, he agreed to go through the motions of spending the night with a prostitute in Brighton. But Diana's father-in-law, Lord Moyne, had other ideas. Lord Moyne secretly hired private detectives to watch Diana's every move; she found it all very amusing and commented: 'It is really rather heavenly to feel that they are around, no pick pockets can approach.' Ostracised from good society, Diana quipped, 'I'm not entertaining at all, but living in a very, very quiet retirement.'

Nancy based all of her fictional work on her family and close friends. Life at the family home might have been unbearably boring, but at least she spawned famous character studies of her loved ones, which she turned into best-selling novels. 'She's not inventive, merely a very good reporter,' Deborah reflected on Nancy's storytelling.

Unity, who was a rather 'large and alarming debutante', had entered the busy season of coming out. During a fleeting spell of boredom at the initial debutante dance at Buckingham Palace, Unity slipped off to a state room and pinched the writing paper, which she used to pen her thank-you notes on. She also draped herself in costume jewels and wore a phony tiara adorned with rubies. In *avant-garde* moments, she cut an exotic figure when she wore her pet grass snake, Enid, coiled around her neck. And, just as things were getting into full swing, Unity would unleash her pet rat, Ratular, from her evening bag and set him loose across the dance floor.

When Deborah was a teenager, she and Muv travelled to Germany via Austria. In Austria, Deborah noticed a boy playing in a band and instantly fell in love with him. On their arrival in Germany, Unity immediately brought them to meet Hitler. Hitler held little intrigue for the lovelorn Deborah. However, she did notice Hitler's monogrammed towels, much like the towels at the Savoy, and that he excessively rang a service bell but nobody answered. Here was the most important man in Germany, Deborah thought, and nobody would answer his calls. Muv, however, had an enjoyable time. Through Unity, serving as translator, Muv and Hitler had a lively chat on the virtues of wholemeal bread. Decades later, an interviewer asked Deborah who she found more interesting, Hitler or Elvis. Deborah retorted, 'Why, Elvis, of course! What an extraordinary question!'

—*∿∿*—

THE MITFORD GUIDE

TO TRICKY SITUATIONS

Sometimes in life there are certain situations which are simply unavoidable. Of course, one can channel Muv and bury one's head in the sand, pretend nothing is wrong, or one can move through life in an 'ignorance is bliss' state of mind. But like it or not, these situations do arise. Just how would the Mitfords cope with potentially volatile situations? First thing's first, let's look at the root of all problems.

ARGUMENTS

The Mitfords were not without their fair share of disagreements, which were usually conducted through their endless letters. How does one conduct an argument Mitford style? It always helps if wires are crossed and misunderstandings are blown out of proportion.

Begin the argument by writing a letter to the opponent and close with 'I am going on holiday', even if you are actually staying at home. This will provide some light entertainment for you, and annoy the recipient. The recipient will reply to the letter, usually in an impulsive fury.

Jessica always kept carbon copies of her correspondence, which is a clever idea as she had both sides to the story, so to speak. When you receive the letter, do not respond right away; remember you are supposed to be elsewhere. Leave it for a week or two and then respond with a chatty letter as though nothing had happened. The recipient will be eagerly awaiting a response, probably expecting the worst and are fired up for a full-blown fight. Imagine how surprised and confused they will be to discover that you have moved on.

In letters, Jessica was persistent with her point of view. If the outcome of an argument was not to her satisfaction, she would relentlessly pursue her case, despite her sisters hedging her off. The Mitfords loved to play with people, and arguments were no exception. Everything was a figure of fun, or to coin Nancy's unique phrase, 'sick-making'.

I am, of course, drawing on the infamous scrapbook argument of 1976, when Pamela wrote to Jessica accusing her of stealing Muv's precious scrapbook which Deborah kept at Chatsworth. Jessica, like anybody who has been accused of theft, was furious. She wrote to Deborah and accused her and Diana of using Pamela as their go-between.

Pamela closed her letter with news of her immediate Swiss holiday and informed Jessica of her prolonged absence, should she wish to reply. Deborah, on the other hand, refused to apologise and only settled the argument months later with a short telegram exclaiming, 'Eureka', referring to the appearance of the missing scrapbook.

This quarrel went on for a decade, with Jessica recalling the incident whenever she felt short-changed by Deborah, often smugly (and rightly so) adding that she was, in fact, innocent. About ten years later, Jessica's husband Bob took the opportunity to ask Deborah about the scrapbook as he escorted her to the car. Deborah refused to acknowledge the past incident and concluded the conversation with a cryptic, 'Goodbye, Bob', as she sped away. Eventually, after much prompting from Jessica, Deborah apologised.

The girls channelled their own unique responses and reacted accordingly to heated situations:

- *Diana*, when displeased, would slowly close her eyes and turn away.
- *Pamela*, when angry, would turn scarlet and her eyes would well up with tears.
- *Nancy* would thrive on the cattiness of an argument and fire out witty responses.
- *Unity* would slide under the table and only emerge when the coast was clear.
- *Jessica* would fight her cause until she received a satisfactory outcome.
- *Deborah* would refrain from arguing whenever possible. But, as Jessica stated, Deborah could leave one in no doubt of her feelings by simply saying nothing. Her cold facial expression said it all.

For an immediate effect, one should aim to speak in what is known as the 'Mitford drawl' – a slow slurring of the words which should come across as vacant and without feeling. That ought to do the trick.

BIRTHDAYS

It is the one anniversary which everyone can rest assured will pop up once a year. With six girls in the family, born almost two decades apart, milestone birthdays came around more often than the average family. In Mitford years, 18 was the special age because it meant the girls were officially ready for marriage.

Nancy often 'forgot' about birthdays. She claimed she could never remember dates and promised to invest in a birthday book to record such anniversaries. She never did. Was this a cost-effective way for Nancy to escape buying presents?

CHRISTMAS

Christmas cards are such a nightmare to me.
— Nancy

The lead up to Christmas is always stressful, and even more so for whoever is hosting the festivities. Follow the Mitford lead, and always write months in advance to whoever you plan to spend the festive season with. Usually such gatherings, if large, should be held in a spacious house such as Chatsworth, which meant Deborah was often the host during the holidays. A vacant castle is also an option.

Nancy would always complain about going to England – 'How one dreads it' – and debate whether or not such a journey would be worth it. Of course, she always showed up, but continued to complain.

Pamela, too, would write in advance to ponder the treacherous weather: would there be snow, how could one drive in such conditions and would such a trip be worthy of putting one's life at risk? This would infuriate and amuse the other girls because it was so typical of Pamela to create a saga (she was famous for them) and then show up without a glitch.

It is always a good idea to check in advance whether one should exchange gifts or not. Pamela often made a rule of 'No Presents' because she would be transporting household supplies, in bulk, from Switzerland to England.

Don't forget to write thank-you notes to the people who have sent you gifts. Pamela had little patience for those who did not express gratitude. In 1975, Jessica had luncheon with Pamela who spent the entire time complaining about Deborah's young grandchildren: 'I sent presents up to Chatsworth in plenty of time for Christmas Eve,' and she pointed out it was 3 January and not one recipient had said thank you. Jessica reminded Pamela that the children were about 3 years old and probably hadn't learned how to write yet. But that did not faze Pamela; she expected a thank you, nonetheless.

How to Do the Mitford Childhood Christmas

- Buy one's siblings' presents from the stationery shop Packers.
- Craft something by hand for one's parents such as a beaded tray cloth or an embroidered anti-massacre.
- Exchange presents before the others delve into their Christmas stockings. In the style of Jessica, if one dislikes one's presents or deems them unnecessary, don't be afraid to sell them on to one's relatives.
- Don't be afraid to dispose of an unwanted gift.
- On Christmas night, indulge in a fancy dress dinner. One must not buy anything or prepare in advance, as this is a test of one's resourcefulness. Pamela always appeared Christmas after Christmas as Lady Rowena from *Ivanhoe*, in a purple dress, accessorised with wooden beads.
- After everyone has been decked out in their fancy dress finery, it is a good idea to take a group photograph using the self-timer.

➤ Conclude the evening with a spot of light entertainment, such as a game of Commerce which should be played for money prizes. But do be mindful of Farve's rules:
  1. No elbows on the card table.
  2. No talking during the game.
➤ Last but not least, as the evening's festivities draw to a close, provide baskets for guests to transport their loot.

GIFTS

In terms of gift giving, it is best to follow Diana's lead. Buy a simple gift which is not too flashy or obvious in its wealth, but do make it personal; the recipient should immediately recognise the thought that has gone into the gift, and the meaning, if any, behind it. It does not have to be an expensive gift, and in the style of Diana, do play down its worth: 'The present was mingy beyond belief; I rather wish it had got lost in the post.'

When viewing her wedding presents, which consisted of vast collections of vases, valuable silver, china and glass, Diana's mother-in-law, Lady Evelyn, gazed at the display and whispered, 'The glass is the easiest; it only needs a good kick.' Farve was disappointed at the display of ungratefulness and he brought Diana down to earth when he reproachfully reminded her, 'People are very kind to give you presents.'

Sometimes receiving a gift can be a bad thing. One Christmas Diana presented a small gift to Nancy, who eagerly tore off the wrapping paper. Dissatisfied with the gift, she tossed it into the fire without giving it a second glance. Diana was 'grateful' for Nancy's honesty.

DEBUTANTE DANCES

I have never seen anything like the collection of young men – all completely chinless.

– Deborah on her dancing partners

As the girls would say, 'viz' a small square room to dance in, with too many people crammed in the doorway and along the staircase. And debutantes dressed in long white dresses of silk and tulle, fitted bodice, thin straps and a flared skirt. No bare shoulders. Opera-length gloves were sent to Edinburgh to be laundered, so extra care was taken to keep them clean. Hair was kept simple and neat, nothing too elaborate: remember, one had to look virginal in order to snare a good husband. Make-up was not too flashy but red lipstick was a must. Jewels were kept simple; pearls were a safe option, and only married women could get away with wearing diamonds and the family tiara, which was centuries old and often dusty from its lifeless existence in an ancient bank vault.

Often the debutantes would know one another, or have a cousin or family friend who was coming out at the same time. But sometimes they might have been at a dance where they knew nobody, only their parents, who would be seated off to the side with the other grown-ups. Of course, one had to be U (upper-class) about it and put on a brave face despite having a perfectly awful time. Awkwardness was a rite of passage at a deb dance. And keeping with tradition, the young man, known as a 'Chinless Wonder', always approached the girl to ask for a dance. A typical conversation would follow:

Chinless Wonder: I think this is our dance …

The debutante would check her dance card to confirm.

Young Deb: Oh yes, I believe it is.

At this stage in the conversation the young man would take the deb's arm and escort her on to the dance floor.

Chinless Wonder: What a crowd in the doorway!
Young Deb: Yes, isn't it awful?

The young man, in a moment of confidence, would then clumsily clutch the debutante by her waist. She would almost fall over as she tried to put her feet where his weren't.

Young Deb: Sorry!
Chinless Wonder: No, my fault.
Young Deb: Oh, I think it must have been me!
Chinless Wonder: Oh no, that wouldn't be possible. [This should be taken as a compliment.]

After a brief but polite conversation, an uncomfortable silence ensued; dancing became too unbearable, the small talk had run out and the debutante's toes were just about crushed to death. Finally, they would both telepathically decide to sit down and, as if by a miracle, the drums rolled to signify the end of the dance. As they made their way to the door, the debutante would hear the same 'funny' story three times.

Debo was very amusing, and very beautiful and therefore very popular. She almost always wore tulle dresses with large crinolines, which made her stand out as that was an unusual style for the 1930s.

– Lady Lloyd, a fellow debutante

A debutante's day often began early in the morning with hair appointments, dress fittings and the timely ordeal of getting dressed and putting on one's face. Diana recalled Nancy's stamina during the debutante season: 'When she came out she often danced all night and hunted all day and danced again. She stayed in countless country houses and someone who really lacked energy would have collapsed after these exertions.'

If a debutante had a free afternoon, she could often manage to take a nap in between the morning and evening dances. Despite the glamour associated with the season, the debutante's schedule was gruelling and often they had no time to eat.

To ward off any offending hunger pangs, Jessica stuffed chocolates into her bouquet of flowers to snack on between dances. However, the chocolates rolled out on to the floor during Jessica's photo session, leaving her red faced and rather unsophisticated looking.

I am not a debutante wondering what balls she will get invited to; people can take me or leave me.

– Diana

PET HATES

It's much more painful to hate than to be hated.

– Diana

NANCY

Nancy was easily irritated and extremely vocal about her likes and dislikes. Her pet hates, usually trivial, are just as well remembered as her fictional novels. They were, in no particular order:

- Her brothers-in-law, especially Sir Oswald, whom she referred to as 'Sir Ogre'.
- Store-bought clothes and short boxy jackets.
- When rich American tourists, dressed in their beach clothes, invaded Paris and congregated at her favourite haunt, the Ritz.
- Ignore the above. Nancy loathed *all* Americans whether or not they were rich tourists.
- The British Royal Family. Nancy thought their dress sense was appalling and a poor representation of the British people who looked up to their monarch for inspiration.
- New money.
- Travelling home to England.
- Swinbrook House, which she nicknamed 'Swinebook'.
- Housework.

PAMELA

As much as Nancy's pet hates were trivial, Pamela's dislikes were mainly from an economical point of view. Usually calm and serene, nothing riled her more than:

- Wasting food and natural resources, i.e. water.
- Squandering money.
- Driving in the snow (she drove from Switzerland to England and vice versa).

🐦 Small children.

🐦 The hassle of buying Christmas presents and not receiving a gesture of thanks, especially from small children.

DIANA

Diana was quite level-headed in her dislikes. They were quite basic and easily relatable:

🐦 As most people do as they get older, Diana deplored nightclubs, finding them to be boring and a waste of time. She said: 'We used to go to nightclubs to annoy our parents really. I never enjoyed them. It was considered rather slow not *ever* to go to a nightclub.'

🐦 Negativity towards Sir Oswald and anyone who dared to have a different point of view from his.

🐦 Arguments induced her into floods of tears and unfairness angered her.

🐦 On a more trivial note, aeroplane delays really irritated her.

UNITY

Ironically, unlike her behaviour, Unity's dislikes were very predictable and can be summarised in a few key notes:

🐦 Communists.

🐦 Negativity towards Hitler: 'Poor sweet Führer, he's having such a dreadful time.'

🐦 Abroad (Germany is not included as she felt at one with the people).

🐦 The 'affected' French language.

🐦 Debutantes.

JESSICA

Jessica stuck to her moral code and made no excuses for her dislikes. In no particular order, they were:

- Diana.
- Racism.
- Fascism.
- Nazism.
- The Conservative Party.
- The aristocracy.
- Petty rules.

DEBORAH

Although quite placid, nothing upset Deborah more than:

- Attending school.
- Playing a game of tennis.
- Having Tony Blair in government.
- Discussing the class system.

AVOIDING TEMPTATION:

MITFORD STYLE

Like Wilde I can resist anything except temptation – but I was never in the slightest degree tempted.

— Diana

Nancy was the first sister to dabble in the vices of modern life, and whilst cooped up at Swinbrook, the younger Mitfords breathlessly related recollections of Nancy smoking a cigarette, Nancy playing the ukulele which was so fashionable at the time, Nancy going to nightclubs, Nancy having young men to stay, Nancy going abroad. For a short time, it was a never-ending social whirl at Swinbrook, which infuriated Farve who was as anti-social as they come. 'Damned sewer,' he would hiss at the congregation of Bright Young Things as they passed through the front door.

How would the girls hold up against today's modern vices? One must draw upon their own experiences during their youth and apply it to certain delicate topics which are so acceptable in today's society. Would the Mitfords ...

GET DRUNK?

Unlike the Bright Young Things and daring debutantes of their day, the girls did not indulge in heavy drinking, with the exception of Jessica who developed alcoholism and addressed the problem in her later years. Nancy drank alcohol for 'medicinal' purposes and kept whisky in her flat to be consumed by her guests. But in their youth the girls did not indulge in excessive drinking at all.

STEAL?

The Mitfords had an eccentric governess named Miss Bunting, who would ask, 'Like to try a little jiggery-pokery, children?' Jiggery-pokery was the code name for shoplifting. The children would accompany Miss Bunting to the local village shops, where they would indulge in the petty crime. There were two main methods of shoplifting, as described by Jessica in *Hons and Rebels*:

> *The Shopping Bag Method*: An accomplice was needed to distract the shopkeeper while the appointed jiggery-poker stuffed books, underclothes or boxes of chocolate into the shopping bag.
>
> *The Dropped Hanky Method*: This method of shoplifting was best suited for pilfering small objects, such as lipstick or small pieces of jewellery.

Afterwards, Miss Bunting, Unity, Jessica and Deborah would stroll past the unsuspecting shop assistants to the safety of a Fullers tea room, where they would gleefully admire each other's loot.

Petty theft also united the two politically opposed sisters. One afternoon, Unity and Jessica were helping Muv on her produce stall at the Conservative fête when Jessica mischievously shook the kitty and remarked, 'Look at all this money. It does seem a shame to think of the beastly old Conservatives getting it.' Unity snatched half of the takings and said she was sending it to the British Union of Fascists. In return, Jessica pinched the rest of the money and said she was sending her share to the *Daily Worker*, a communist magazine which she subscribed to. They met on common ground when each stole a share of their mother's takings in order to help support their political parties.

Adultery

I find this guessing about the sex life of friends or relations tiresome in the extreme.

– Deborah

Visualise the scene: the 1920s debutante dances, where young women from aristocratic families were paraded in front of the best of high society for the duration of the social season, with one aim, to be married off. Love or mutual attraction did not come into the equation; it was all about getting the girls financially secure, and in return they would carry out their duty and provide an heir. 'Marriage was the career that we all aspired to, we were not trained to do a paid job,' Deborah said.

Adultery has always been rife among the aristocracy, and it was an acceptable way to live in the Mitfords' era, for once an heir was provided many spouses went their separate ways and did not risk the social stigma that divorce brought. However, adultery was only acceptable if it was carried out discreetly.

> *She [Cimmie] and Mosley both seemed so much older than me, and so much more experienced. Kit [her name for Mosley] had had so many affairs, and everyone knew – ten or twelve at least that everyone knew about – so I really didn't think she'd mind. What difference would it make?*
>
> – Diana

Diana's public indiscretion with Sir Oswald was met with disdain. Had she quietly continued to see him and remained with her husband, at least in name only, things might have been different. Scandal, however, tarnished her reputation and she fell out of favour with her once good friends. Bryan pined for Diana and offered to take her back, if only for the sake of her reputation. She rejected his kind offer and persevered with her lonely life of waiting for Sir Oswald, who would stroll to Diana's house from his flat located around the corner on Ebury Street. To signal his arrival, he would quietly tap on her drawing room window with his cane.

Diana sacrificed everything to be with Sir Oswald and her public reputation never recovered. Although behind closed doors she was lovable 'Aunt Honks' to her many nieces and nephews, to this day the very mention of her name conjures up images of Hitler and the atrocities of the Second World War.

The moral of the story is that Diana threw away her lot to be with Sir Oswald and she never regretted it. She decided that public and personal backlash was worth it as she set down that long and complicated road that became her life.

The only thing wrong with it was the men in her life, they were hopeless.

– Diana on Nancy's fabled love life

Nancy lived a miserable existence due to her affair with Charles de Gaulle's right-hand man, Colonel Gaston Palewski. Unlike Sir Oswald, who had feelings for Diana, Gaston never claimed to love Nancy and he carefully strung her along during their relationship in Paris. He could not afford to treat Nancy to the grandees in life, and often she dined alone because he could not afford to pay the bill and, unlike her husband, was too proud to accept a handout. Nancy craved glamour and romance, but instead she got a husband who stole her money and, as she saw him, a lover who used to throw her whatever scraps of time he could spare. She was unlucky in love and channelled her energies into writing farcical novels on the subject. See The Mitford Guide to Falling Love (p. 142).

HAVE CHILDREN OUT OF WEDLOCK?

In those days it was supposed to be better for children to be born in wedlock.

– Diana

In all stations of the class system, illegitimacy was enough to ostracise one from society. The girls' maternal grandfather, Tap Gibson Bowles, had been the illegitimate son of an early Victorian Cabinet minister, Milner Gibson. Nobody knew anything about his mother except that her name was Susan Bowles. The girls tried to find out information about their great-grandmother but to no avail; Diana wrote: 'She was swallowed up in the mists of time.' Fortunately for Tap, his father's wife loved the boy and he was brought up in their family, but due to his illegitimacy, he went to school in France.

In the early days of her affair with Sir Oswald, Diana became pregnant twice and both times she resorted to having an abortion. It was a criminal act in the 1930s, but an understanding gynaecologist would abort the pregnancy providing it was very early on. Under ordinary circumstances, illegitimacy in those days would have been social suicide for the mother and an even worse fate for the child.

SMOKE?

Nancy might have experimented with cigarettes in the early 1920s, but none of the Mitfords, except for Jessica, were smokers. However, depending on the source, some claimed that a cigarette never passed Nancy's lips, and the tale of 'Nancy smoking a cigarette' was a figment of Jessica's imagination. Smoking was definitely Non-U.

SWEAR?

If you even say 'damn' she [Unity] gets quite furious and says it is wicked to swear.

– Deborah

In an off-guard moment, Deborah swore at Muv. It was a reaction prompted by the tense atmosphere of Unity's unpredictable behaviour following her suicide attempt. Farve shook Deborah so violently that it startled her.

Jessica was the only one to use rough language. It would have been viewed as awfully Non-U to swear, and despite their teases and sometimes bad behaviour, the Mitfords were always impeccably mannered and were not accustomed to using foul words for effect.

—◦◦◦—

THE MITFORD GUIDE TO SOCIETY

Snobbishness was, surely, by definition a purely middle class attribute.

—Jessica

As young children, the Mitfords belonged to a charitable organisation known as The Sunbeams. The Sunbeams was founded on the idea that a rich child would correspond with a poor child, and occasionally send the disadvantaged child hand-me-down clothes and toys. Once, Nancy lost the address to her Sunbeam penpal and simply addressed the envelope to: 'Tommy Jones, The Slums, London.' 'Much to the fury of Nanny, who didn't think it was at all nice,' Jessica wrote in *Hons and Rebels*.

Jessica's Sunbeam was a girl named Rose Dickson. Jessica threw herself into corresponding with Rose; she took great care in selecting her cast-off clothing and spent all of her pocket money on buying presents for her. She imagined her letters, 'which consisted of a highly romanticized account of life at Swinbrook', as being the highlight of her 'otherwise drab existence'. Rose enjoyed receiving the letters and in return her letters were equally fascinating, written in a 'flowery language' with phonetic spelling.

Rose related to Jessica that she was one of six children and described 'in heart rendering detail' the squalor in which her family lived, 'all six of them in two beds in one tiny room'. Jessica was obsessed with the idea of rescuing Rose from her Dickensian life and pleaded with Muv to let her visit Swinbrook. 'I don't think that would do, little D,' Muv explained to Jessica. 'Think of how dreadfully *uncomfortable* she'd feel.' A short while later, Muv decided that it might be best to hire Rose, now 14, as a between maid or 'tweeny'.

'It's like a fairytale come true,' Rose answered. Muv reminded Jessica of the reality of a life in service: 'I'm afraid being a tweeny isn't really much like a fairytale.'

Jessica tried to imagine Rose's appearance, 'probably mere skin and bones, with huge soulful brown eyes'. On the contrary, when they met at the station Jessica was surprised to see she was quite fat, 'but she had the pasty, drawn look of sunless children'. The first meeting resulted in an awkward silence and Jessica was 'relieved' when they reached Swinbrook, where Rose would be handed over to Annie, their parlour maid.

She did not see much of Rose once she had been inducted into her new role. Two days later, Muv broke the sad news: Rose felt homesick and had returned to London.

Jessica had set out with the best intentions to improve Rose's situation, but it was not to be; Rose was simply happier with her family and her surroundings. This lesson proved a catalyst for Jessica to learn the fundamental functions of society.

The ambiguous term 'social climbing' seems very Non-U. According to Jessica, social climbing was typically a middle-class trait: an unhealthy obsession in trying to rise above one's station, to ease oneself up the social ladder, where, according to the social elite, one was not welcome. In return, the middle-class person would look down on those beneath them on the metaphorical social ladder. A complicated matter indeed!

The girls' paternal grandmother would distinguish another person's station in life by asking, 'Is she one of us dear child?' This was not snobbishness on their grandmother's behalf but an enquiry into how one should behave and what one should expect. It was almost as if she were preparing herself for the situation. It has been said that the genuine upper and working classes are far more likeable than new money because they are comfortable within their station; to put it simply, they know no different.

Of course, the Mitfords did not look down on anyone; they stared straight ahead and cared not at all if this limited their vision.

All humans are the same, so there's no point making a great fuss about who is what. It's better for everyone to get together, I reckon.

– Deborah

LEARN THE LINGO

There is nothing so inferior as a gentlewoman who has no French.

– Lady Airlie, the Mitfords' great-grandmother

According to Nancy, as written in her 1955 essay, 'The English Aristocracy', nothing exposed a person's background more than their choice of wording: 'It is true that one U-speaker recognizes another U-speaker almost as soon as he opens his mouth.'

Yes, our voices are so awful. But it's worse for me because they notice it more in the North.

– Deborah

Such affected pronunciation, or the '1930s deb voice', separated the two generations: those born pre-war and those born post-war. Jessica used to play up the use of her Americanisms when visiting the family in England and Nancy in France, who particularly loathed anything American. But Jessica could also revert back to her debutante accent which she used in a mocking tone to amuse her husband and children.

Deborah and Diana also had a talent for dragging out a story without actually reaching the conclusion: 'If you see what I mean … kind of … well, sort of … you know.' And Diana had a unique turn of phrase – 'Vaguely, whoa …' – which she used when certain situations were out of her control. (See Phrases: Mitford Style (p. 162).)

Deborah bemoaned the loss of old-fashioned manners; she felt modern society viewed manners as being 'subservient'. Nothing could be further from the truth, she thought. Old-fashioned manners 'oiled the wheels of relationships', and if one is around people on a daily basis, it simply makes life much more pleasant.

Becoming a Social Pariah

Society can make things pretty beastly to those who disobey its rules.

– Nancy

If one is born into the aristocracy, there seems to be little one can do about one's social standing. After all, what other social rank is there to aspire to, what else can one achieve? Social pariah status, of course!

It is worth noting that, even though one can belong in the highest, most coveted place in the social hierarchy, there is also a fear of not being socially accepted. You see, the class system is quite a fragile commodity, even to those who are born into it, so there is always that niggling fear that one's position could be compromised. If one has done something socially unacceptable – for instance, Diana's relationship with Sir Oswald – one should expect to be shunned from good society.

Although viewed as frivolous, the girls possessed a powerful and unconventional personality, a trait they inherited from Farve. Their toughness was instilled in the nursery and was merely a survival instinct when battling the daily hierarchy of family life. Farve went through phases where he chose a favourite daughter each week; the girls called this 'Rat Week'.

Rat Week meant that somebody would fall out of favour with Farve, and they would be on the receiving end of his wrath, and gestures such as serving them a smaller portion at meal times would highlight just how displeased he was. Nancy's bullying also instilled resilience, and her treatment, likened to mental cruelty, set the girls up for life when dealing with opposition and public backlash.

For those nonconformists who wish to disobey the system, here is a step-by-step guide on how to become a social pariah. Use Diana, Unity or Jessica as your muse. You may use all three but that might result in imprisonment, exile or a fate worse than death (note Unity's bullet in the brain).

DIANA

It was still lovely to wake up in the morning and feel that one was lovely.

– Diana on prison life

Throw in your lot with a kind and well-respected man and set up home with a man who is not only married, but whose reputation is far more notorious than any of his other attributes.

Just as you are on the brink of social exile, make it a point to move into an exclusive area among your social peers, in Diana's case Belgravia. This will not only cause awkwardness when you see your once-feted friends, but it will also set the cat amongst the pigeons, so to speak.

Do make it a point to cheerfully greet each person who privately and publicly scorns you; make direct eye contact and smile sweetly. If spotted from a distance, merrily wave to them. Your opponent's flustered reactions will serve as an amusing dinner party anecdote.

Refrain from relenting in your decision or your loyalty towards your loved one, or your convictions for that matter. This action may be infuriating and puzzling, but at least you cannot be accused of disloyalty.

UNITY

Do not take any social occasion very seriously; use it as an excuse to have fun and, most of all, mock the traditions that go along with it. This is the first step in becoming controversial. When in the presence of the monarchy, or any lofty figure, do seize the opportunity to poke fun at the dress code. Wear a faux gem tiara and lavish costume jewels as an obvious sign of your disregard for pomp and grandeur.

Side with the enemy over everything, but be prepared to suffer the consequences in doing so. Very rarely can one have the best of both worlds. And when questioned over your unsavoury behaviour, never miss a moment to infuriate others. Simply claim that you remember nothing.

After her suicide attempt in 1939, Unity's new obsession became religion. She became a religious fanatic and experimented with a variety of faiths, eventually settling on Christian Science. Avoiding social protocol, Unity would direct inappropriate questions towards the clergymen. Her three favourite questions to ask were:

1. Why did you become a clergyman?
2. Do you wish you had been made a bishop?
3. Do you enjoy sleeping with your wife?

JESSICA

Class was a delicate matter.

– Jessica

Shamelessly run amok through polite society and make it a point to show disregard for anything associated with frivolity, especially the outdated traditions of the upper classes – this always serves as a good catalyst for mockery. Shun well-to-do parties and events in favour of socialising with notorious characters. On that note, make friends with commoners and criminals, and aspire to live in a questionable area.

Make no apologies for your beliefs or actions; remember the gripe is with other people and their sensitive views on your lifestyle are their own problems.

Live openly outside of wedlock, preferably somewhere seedy, such as a cheap hotel or grimy lodgings. And make it your long-term goal to immigrate to a country where the class system is supposedly non-existent, such as America.

Do remember that in such 'classless' countries there is still a social code, so, just to keep your notoriety even on two continents, choose a minority group and tirelessly campaign for their rights.

Last but not least, when you are older and wiser, start exposing lucrative industries for what they are, i.e. the American funeral industry. This muckraking venture should be called 'Investigative Journalism'. See Jessica & *The American Way of Death* (p. 157).

If people are still talking about your wicked, wicked ways years after your demise, you know you have done a good job.

———

DIANA, INCARCERATED

How foul the prison was, how one never stopped dreading the lavatory and so on.

– Diana

Before Diana was arrested in 1940, she was, unbeknownst to her, surveyed by her nearest and dearest for five years. Diana's ex father-in-law, Lord Moyne, asked her Guinness sons' governess, Growler, to spy on her and to report back to him with any evidence of her trips to Germany and talk of Nazism. Growler's most dangerous accusation was discovered among the MI5 papers released in 2002: 'The children would have known how to greet the Führer for they had been taught to give the Nazi salute and to say Heil Hitler.'

MI5 files also revealed that Lord Moyne wrote to the Home Secretary in June 1940, accusing Diana of being an 'extremely dangerous character'. It was enough to arouse suspicions but it seemed MI5 were not overly concerned about Lord Moyne's evidence gathered from a dotty governess.

However, Nancy's meddling had severe consequences. Nancy reported that Diana was 'Far cleverer and dangerous than her husband'. And Nancy used key accusations which were certain to provoke the attention of the Home Secretary. She added that Diana desired the downfall of England and democracy and should not be released: 'She will stick at nothing to achieve her ambitions, is wildly ambitious, a ruthless shrewd egotist, a devoted fascist and admirer of Hitler.'

According to Diana, nothing could have been further from the truth. In *A Life of Contrasts*, she wrote about the autumn of 1939, when Sir Oswald campaigned for peace. Surprisingly, a large amount of the public supported his plea for peace and, a far cry from the orchestrated violence of the BUF days in the early 1930s, the audience listened with the 'strangest' response. They stood in silence until he had finished speaking and then erupted into riotous applause. Sir Oswald asked them to raise their arms for peace.

In the spring of 1940, just eight months after war had been declared, MI5 ordered the arrest of Diana and Sir Oswald under Regulation 18B. The regulations of 18B stated that anybody could be imprisoned without charge, hence no trial, by the Home Secretary for as long as he saw fit; it was, as Diana said, 'Exactly like being kidnapped.'

Churchill was initially enthusiastic about Regulation 18B – 'A grotesque notion', Diana wrote – however, as time went on he began to question whether Regulation 18B was in line with his role of a democrat fighting the Nazis' totalitarian state. Three years had passed since Diana had been arrested when Churchill denounced Regulation 18B as 'in the highest degree odious' and demanded that it be demolished. However, the Home Secretary had 'become addicted to power' and paid no attention to Churchill's sudden change of heart.

Diana was not the only aristocrat guilty of enjoying a polite friendship with Hitler: many upper-class men and women, dignitaries and public figures were flocking to Germany to meet him. But during a time of great patriotism, it was concluded that, in the best interest of the public, the Mosleys should be imprisoned.

Nancy's actions remained hidden until the 1980s. Diana's daughter-in-law, Charlotte Mosley, was editing a volume of Nancy's letters for the book *Love from Nancy* when she discovered the secret in her private letters to close friends.

Nancy deplored Nazism and fascism, and held strong views against her brother-in-law's political ideology. She could tolerate Unity's childish devotion to Hitler, for she went in for the pageantry of the Nazi rallies. But Nancy felt that Diana, who was the most intelligent out of all the sisters, deserved to be punished because she was more than aware of the sinister elements associated with a fascist regime.

As hypocritical as her actions were, Nancy felt she had done her political duty by informing on Diana. In true Nancy fashion, she wondered what Diana did when the lights went out in her cell. 'Probably thinks of Adolf,' she quipped.

Diana had been feeding her youngest son, Max, who was 11 weeks old when the police came to arrest her. Sir Oswald had already been interned at Brixton Prison under Regulation 18B, but there seemed to be no reason why Diana should be arrested. The police assured Diana that she was being taken away for questioning, a formality at the most, and would be gone for the weekend; she was advised to pack enough clothes to last the duration. Diana said goodbye to baby Max and left him in the nursery with his 19-month-old brother and their nanny.

As Diana was escorted into Holloway Prison she had no idea it would be three and a half years before she would be released. After the humiliating ritual of checking her for lice and other undesirable afflictions, such as venereal disease, she was led to her cell.

The claustrophobic 12ft by 7ft cell had no bed; only a thin, stained mattress lay on the stone floor with a filthy, itchy woollen blanket thrown on top, too scarce to tuck in. The floor was awash with water in an attempt to remove some of the embedded dirt, and the only light came from a 25-watt lightbulb which was promptly switched off at nine o'clock. The cold, even in summer, was constant; no ray of sunlight could shine through the tiny barred windows encrusted with soot. Diana's cell was located on the notorious E wing which also contained the execution shed, and a feeling of fear and uncertainty engulfed the wing.

The smallest gestures which one might take for granted, such as being allowed to wear her own clothes, made her life easier in some ways. Diana made friends with the other inmates and was on friendly terms with some of the prison guards. She never complained and never broke down in front of the others. 'I, who cry easily, never shed a tear when anyone could see it,' she later said. In time, her resilience won her the admiration of her prison mates.

On the outside, Muv appealed to Churchill for Diana's release. Unwilling to interfere with Regulation 18B, Churchill sent a memo to Holloway demanding that Diana be granted a bath every day. Diana, emotionally wrecked, laughed at the pitiful suggestion which was physically impossible with so little water to go around.

Diana purposely avoided using as many of the prison facilities as possible. The eating utensils were coated in grease and, unwilling to consume the disgusting prison food, cooked in large cauldrons and deemed inedible, she survived on a diet of Stilton cheese and port wine. The Stilton was sent in from Harrods, and Diana used the rest of her ration coupons to send her eldest Guinness sons, who were away at boarding school, sweets and other treats. Although Diana lived on a basic diet and obeyed prison rules, she did request a few luxuries from home:

- A few country flowers.
- A Woolworth's cup and saucer.
- A bowl or dish for salad or anything she might be able to cook.
- Cutlery, as the prison utensils were too vile for words.
- Wool for knitting her own clothes.

During her lengthy stay in prison Diana befriended a beautiful German woman who had been granted permission to bring a gramophone into Holloway. She reckoned the German woman was very rich, as she ordered a vast amount of records. With the records she held concerts in a room across the yard. When they became friendly, she asked Diana of her musical preferences and produced a series of recordings: Schubert, Bach, Handel, Debussy and Wagner. 'Despite the tiresome pauses while the gramophone was wound up these concerts were heavenly,' Diana wrote in *A Life of Contrasts*.

The German woman had a peculiarity of carrying her 'amazing jewels' around in a fish basket. When Diana suggested that it might be safer to trust the jewels to the care of the prison warden, the German woman looked at her as though she were mad and tactfully responded, 'How could one trust one's jewels to the lying swine who put an innocent woman in a vile prison?'

In 1941, just over a year after her arrest, Diana and Sir Oswald were interned together on the grounds of Holloway in a parcels house. They shared the space with two other married couples. Their reunion made life bearable, but the uncertainty of their release loomed over them. The Mosleys were permitted two servants in the form of 'clean and honest' sex offenders, one of whom was a convicted bigamist.

Diana made the most of their domestic life together, cooking porridge for Sir Oswald and tending to a small vegetable patch. Occasionally, her two eldest sons were permitted to join their mother and Sir Oswald for supper. Visits with the two youngest children were too upsetting as they would be in hysterics when visiting time was over. Alexander, then 2 years old, would try to hold on to Diana and scream when his nanny took him away. For her youngest sons' emotional well-being, Diana decided to refrain from having them visit her. A painful choice on her behalf for it would be two more years before she would be reunited with them, by which time she had become a stranger to them.

Imprisonment began to take its toll, and already undernourished and pale, Diana caught the gastrointestinal flu that swept through Holloway. Her illness was exasperated by the coldness of the large stone rooms in which they resided. It was November and they would not be allowed to have an open fire until January. Worried that Diana might contract pneumonia, the doctor was sent for and was shocked at the sub-human conditions that she was living in. Diana was dangerously thin and had a subnormal temperature of 97.4°F, with a poor pulse. However, the illness ran its course and she made a full recovery.

In 1943, the Mosleys were released from prison on medical grounds due to Sir Oswald's phlebitis in his left leg. They were placed under house arrest at Pamela's house, and spent the rest of the war years hidden away in the countryside.

Thirty years later, Nancy admitted to Diana: 'Isn't it extraordinary to think that a civilized country like England could put a man in prison for years, who's done nothing? I always thought he was in a plot, everybody did.' Nancy's ironic remark was provoked by two things: her dependence on Diana who was tending to her on her sickbed and the government's release of Cabinet papers which detailed Sir Oswald's arrest and internment. Fortunately for Nancy, her actions had not been exposed.

Sixty years later, Diana was asked by an enquiring journalist, 'What did prison teach you?' and without hesitating, she responded, 'Nothing, except to hate discomfort, which I always have hated.'

DIANA'S GUIDE TO PRISON

Going to prison turned out to be quite a surprise.

— Diana

During Diana's three-year internment, she had a lot of time to reflect on her life and gain skills of self-sufficiency. When the bus pulled up to Holloway Prison, the driver would turn around and call out, 'All change here for Lady Mosley's Suite'. Drawing on Diana's resourcefulness, creativity and strength of character, here is a step-by-step guide on how she survived prison.

- Do sue national newspapers for libel when they publish false information. Contrary to popular belief, Diana was not living a life of luxury in prison with access to her own personal hairdresser and army of servants, nor did she have a private viewing of the latest fashions.
- Do purchase a cheap fur coat with the compensation. This will serve as a blanket as well as a garment, as prison bedding is too revolting for words.
- Do use the repulsive evening treat of congealed hot chocolate as face cream. It will be too thick to drink anyway.
- Tread carefully when selecting a library book from the trolley. The prisoners always selected a book with a red cover because they would apply the dye to their lips as a substitute for lipstick.
- Don't use the lavatories with a red V painted on the door. The queue may be shorter but it could result in venereal disease.

- Do learn a new skill. Diana knitted clothes for herself and her family.
- Don't be ashamed of ordering in food from one's shopping account at Harrods. Diana survived on Stilton and port wine for the duration of her sentence.
- Do take advantage of visitors. Don't be ashamed to ask one's visitors to bring in luxuries from home. Diana requested a knife, a fork and a china cup.
- Don't be above appealing to the prime minister for release, especially if he is family. This might be unattainable, but the prime minister may demand that you receive special privileges, such as a daily bath.
- Do organise a social club and appoint oneself as president. The social club will serve as a cultural hub for like-minded inmates. Listening to gramophone records and playing card games will be sufficient recreational hobbies.
- Do appeal for a room of one's own.
- Do make a house a home. Diana and Sir Oswald were eventually permitted to live together in the parcels house alongside two other married couples. Diana's two eldest sons were permitted to dine regularly with their mother and Sir Oswald.
- Don't refuse domestic help.
- Do plan your exit. Naturally, due to the bad press Diana and Sir Oswald had attracted over the years, their release from prison created a public outcry and was delayed due to the crowds of protesters. Diana and Sir Oswald were bundled into a police car and removed from prison in the early hours of the morning.

It's the Garden of Eden out there, Lady Mosley in her little knickers.

–A visiting priest to a prison warden

FAN DEVOTION: A CAUTIONARY TALE

When one sits beside him, it's like sitting beside the sun. He gives out rays or something.

– Unity on Hitler

In 1933 Unity was an eccentric 19-year-old who possessed a desire to shock the world and provoke reactions in people; often they passively suffered her childish displays of foolishness, which further encouraged her, until one day she went a step too far. Not content with being a very vocal member of the British Union of Fascists (it was a proud day whenever Sir Oswald first met Unity and exclaimed, 'Hello Fascist!') she decided she should like to visit Germany, with one intention: to meet Hitler.

Ruthless in her quest to find Hitler, Unity scoured his favourite haunts around Munich. Today she would be arrested for stalking, but Hitler had most of Germany under his wicked spell, and Unity was merely viewed as another smitten fan. Unity lunched at Hitler's favourite restaurant, the Ostaria Bavaria, where she sat at the same table day in day out, staring at him.

She could not believe her luck when, a year later, Hitler finally invited her over for luncheon. The meeting would be 'the most wonderful and beautiful day' of her life. Besotted by her introduction to Hitler, Unity declared that she would not mind dying as all of her dreams had come true.

Unity edged her way into Hitler's inner circle and made a note in her diary each time they met, which totalled 140 times over the space of four years. Sarah Norton, a fellow debutante, remembered: 'We used to see Unity having tea and gaping at Hitler. We just thought she was a bit barmy.'

This obsession took over her life and, on the day England announced war with Germany, Unity took her pearl-handled pistol, a gift from Hitler, placed it to her temple and pulled the trigger.

Unity may have been the mistress of her own fate, but her unhealthy obsession with Hitler did, indeed, ruin her life. After her clumsy suicide attempt she lived for a further eight years as a virtual invalid with the mentality of a 12-year-old.

UNITY'S GUIDE TO IDOL WORSHIP ... OR STALKING

I prefer to be called a Nationalist Socialist, as you know.

– Unity to Jessica, 1937

♥ At first, do be discreet as not everyone will understand your devotion and others may view it as an unhealthy pastime. Disregard those individuals and, if necessary, banish them from your life.

♥ Don't scrimp on fan merchandise: posters, figurines and other cheap souvenirs will keep one's morale up.

♥ Devise a fool-proof plan to relocate somewhere within close proximity to your idol. Something educational or work-related is a good alibi.

♥ Don't allow barriers to stand in the way: people, sea, land or language.

♥ Do learn the native language at once and aim to be fluent.

♥ Do adopt the culture of the one you adore.

♥ Do scour the local haunts that your idol frequents. Become a regular at such establishments, incognito at first.

♥ Do become friendly with the staff. Once their trust has been gained, it will be easy to figure out a rough schedule of when your idol drops by.

♥ Don't become too obvious or legal documents may appear in your letterbox.

♥ Do note the number of idol sightings. This will keep spirits up and also establish a pattern of sightings: where, what, when etc.

♥ Don't rush head first into an encounter with your idol as this will label you as another fan. Edge your way in slowly and discreetly.

♥ Do make eye contact and ensure you are noticed on a daily basis; eventually this may lead to an introduction.

♥ Do be casual and behave indifferently during the introduction, which may only last five seconds. Playing it cool will give you an edge; it will make your idol comfortable in your presence and may lead to further small meetings.

Revenge, Unity Style

She was lawless, completely.

– Diana on Unity

Unity had a childish notion of getting revenge on those who caused her annoyance. This is best displayed through her joyful subscription of the high-society magazine *Tatler*. Unity and Hitler would flick through the society pages, with her pointing out which aristocrat deserved to be shot, and she went so far to devise a list. Needless to say, Hitler had much more sinister things on his mind than ransacking a debutante ball.

In 1934, Muv travelled to Munich to visit Unity, and they embarked on a sightseeing tour of the city with Unity serving as her tour guide. It was a ridiculous rule that one had to salute a Nazi memorial as they passed by, and Unity noticed that Muv refrained from doing so. Wondering if Muv was unaware of the rule, Unity brought her past the statue once again via a different route and, again, Muv did not salute.

Unity was offended and sought revenge by jumping into a passing tram, thus leaving Muv, not knowing a word of German, to find her own way back to the hotel. Unity proudly noted that she abandoned Muv in the morning and it took until dinner time for her to find her way home. Unity was rather pleased and thought this was a sufficient punishment.

Unity was apparently one of the few people who, in Hitler's company, could speak out and say what she thought. I think she was rather like the court jester.

– Charlotte Mosley

EXTREMIST BEHAVIOUR

So terribly pathetic, it really makes one miserable to see her.

– Deborah on Unity's appearance after the suicide attempt

Unity's devotion to Nazism was not at all strange in Germany, where wearing a Nazi badge was the norm and a sign of devotion towards Hitler. Those who refused to conform to the Nazi regime were subjected to severe beatings. Unity was not one of those poor individuals.

Unity paraded around Hyde Park wearing her swastika badge, a gift from Hitler, pinned to the lapel of her jacket. In England, leanings towards Nazism and Sir Oswald's British Union of Fascists were severely frowned upon and those who caught sight of Unity wearing her badge reacted with violence. A crowd, who were protesting against fascism, noticed Unity's badge and attacked her. The police had to intervene. Unity, not at all dismayed by the attack, brightly told a newspaper:

They kicked me, spat at me, screamed insults and threatened to duck me in the pond. The Führer does not mind men getting mixed up in shindies, but he does not like women being involved, as he thinks it undignified. I am afraid he may be cross with me.

– Milwaukee Journal, 24 June 1938

Diana believed that Unity was the first in the family to suffer as a result of the war. Unity's patriotic love of Germany and England had caused her to act extremely following the announcement of war. The bullet lodged in Unity's skull erased any familiar traces of her once-vibrant personality. What remained was a shell of a person, and although outsiders claimed to see a massive improvement in Unity's health, the family was left with a stranger to care for. In true Nancy fashion, she remarked that it was 'poetic justice' for the suffering Unity's Nazi friends had inflicted upon millions of innocent people.

She told me that if there was a war, which of course we all terribly hoped there might not be, that she would kill herself because she couldn't bear to live and see these two countries tearing each other to pieces, both of which she loved.

– Diana

Unity's physical looks were said to be 'the personification of an Aryan woman'. Unity's features resembled Diana's, although warped, as though one was looking at Diana's reflection in a cracked mirror. She had enormous eyes of pale blue and flaxen blonde hair cut into a severe bob, often worn straight or with a slight wave, which emphasised her strong jaw line. Like Diana, she had a flat forehead, straight nose and pronounced chin, and judging from their striking profiles, they could have been twins.

After her suicide attempt, Unity's features were unrecognisable and a cruel reminder of the suffering she had inflicted upon herself. Her complexion was dull, her eyes pale and sunk into her head, and her teeth were yellow and rotting. Her hair had turned grey and was matted with blood from the bullet wound. Her left side was paralysed and she could barely string a sentence together. Deborah, the first sister to see her, was shocked and saddened by the pathetic imposter who claimed to be Unity.

Once she [Unity] asked me, 'Do you think I'm mad?' I said yes of course darling Bonehead but then you always were.

– Nancy

The British newspapers were printing daily reports on Unity's time in Germany. Nobody issued a press release to confirm that she had attempted suicide and the tabloids were surmising all kinds of elaborate scenarios, one of them being that Unity, after a quarrel with Hitler, had drunk poison to end her life. Unity's friend, G. Ward Price, published his own version of events which differ greatly to the monstrous portrait of her that was painted by the press:

She is feminine to the point of being almost old fashioned. There is nothing about her of the sappy, cynical, up-to-date young woman who smokes a lot of cigarettes and drinks many cocktails. Miss Mitford's blue eyes and milk-white complexion give to her an innocence of appearance that is almost child-like. She has a drawling, musical voice and an unsophisticated manner that is rather mid-Victorian than

*Neo-Georgian. She never smokes or drinks.
I believe she does not eat meat either, and except
for the ardour of her political opinions one would
say that she was unusually modest. One quality
which no one can deny to her is courage, and with
it goes a headstrong will. Misguided as her
enthusiasm for Hitler has proved to be, she has
paid dearly for it. Apparently she has been ill
and alone, cut off from her family in an enemy
country since the outbreak of war.*

G. Ward Price, 'In Defence of Unity Mitford', *Vancouver*
9 January 1940

Although Unity never fully recovered, she was permitted to return home after an unsuccessful operation to remove the bullet. Muv decided it was best to take Unity to Old Mill Cottage, the Mitfords' new residence in High Wycombe, which they moved to after Farve could no longer afford the expense of running Swinbrook House. Startled by Unity's transformation, her loved ones found it 'extraordinary and horrifying' to witness not only the physical changes which ravaged her innocent looks, but the personality transformation too. She adopted stages of doing things, very slowly and meticulously, like a child, and she got into the habit of standing up until everyone in the room had sat down and became furious if anyone started eating before Muv. Previously on friendly terms with one another, Unity developed a strong hatred towards Deborah and physically attacked her on more than one occasion. Living at home became a gruelling ordeal for everyone.

*I also remember being shocked by the vacant
smile and orange teeth ... How cruel it was,
really, to bring her back to life.*

– Deborah

Farve, who was fastidious by nature, became irritated by Unity's clumsiness. He could tolerate Unity no longer and moved to Redesdale Cottage in Northumberland, taking Margaret Wright, the housekeeper from Rutland Gate, with him. Farve and Margaret were to remain a couple until his death in 1958.

Shortly after Farve's departure, Deborah married Lord Andrew Cavendish and left home. With Farve away and their marriage existing in name only, Muv shouldered the burden of caring for Unity. Pamela offered Muv a little respite from time to time by inviting Unity to stay with her, and Nancy sometimes treated Unity to luncheon and kept her overnight. Jessica, who was in America, was kept up to date with Unity's condition and she blamed Diana for it. Diana was of little help as she was imprisoned shortly after Unity's return to England in 1940.

After the war, Muv brought Unity to live on Inch Kenneth, her private island off the coast of Mull. Unity's days were filled by writing short, enthusiastic letters to Diana. 'Oh Nard! Oh Nard!' they usually began, followed by a girlish exclamation: 'I long to see you! Oh Nard!' The senseless letters are an indication of Unity's attention span, which tried the patience of those who loved her. She also filled her days by conducting church services among the chapel ruins on Inch Kenneth to an invisible congregation. Another side effect of Unity's suicide attempt was incontinence, and every morning, without fail, Muv laundered her bed sheets; a daily ritual which she carried out until the end of Unity's life.

Before Nancy moved to Paris, she wrote to Diana to express her concern over who should care for Unity after Muv's death, helpfully adding that she, Diana and Pamela could afford to contribute a pound a week towards her upkeep. Nancy need not have worried. After a short illness in 1948, Unity died on her way to hospital. The cause of death was meningitis, provoked by the old bullet wound which had become infected. Unity's funeral was described by Diana as 'The saddest day of my life'.

Farve's Loyalty

Farve was disappointed in Unity's support of Hitler, and in the beginning he was furious with Diana for taking Unity to Germany. 'I suppose you know,' his angry letter read, 'without being told how absolutely horrified Muv and I were to think of you and Bobo accepting any form of hospitality from people we regard as a murderous gang of pests.' However, Farve, in true Mitford fashion, remained publicly loyal to Unity. Press interviews from 1940 serve as an example of his staunch loyalty: 'I was not ashamed of anything my daughter has done in Germany. I know that all she has done has been done because she thought it would encourage friendship between the two countries.' In fact, Farve rather resented the constant attention Unity attracted from the press.

'One other matter which I find very wounding is that I am constantly described as a Fascist. I am not, never have been, and am not likely to become a Fascist.' Farve, although he condemned Sir Oswald and Diana's affair and never converted to being a card-carrying fascist, was briefly impressed by Hitler's transformation of the German economy. This view, however, dimmed in 1939, when Hitler breeched appeasement and invaded Czechoslovakia.

Farve, who was short of cash at that present time, gallantly refused an offer from top newspapers to give an interview on Unity. 'I have been offered £5000 for a statement but I would not accept £25,000. I have got her home now and that is all that matters.'

DEBO LOVES ELVIS

He was very agile, wonderful movement, wonderful timing and the best voice any of us ever heard.

– Deborah on Elvis

It is no secret that Deborah idolised Elvis Presley. This obsession came about during an unremarkable afternoon in the 1980s, when Deborah switched the television channel and discovered a programme of Elvis in concert. She became enthralled, entranced and instantly fell in love with the deceased king of rock 'n' roll, 'alas not when he was alive', and suddenly realised she was in 'the presence of a genius'.

She made several pilgrimages to Graceland, his home in Tennessee. People began to notice her fixation and started to send her things in the post. She received various pieces of memorabilia, such as temporary Elvis tattoos, Elvis cups, Elvis earrings, Elvis slippers, Elvis postcards and books. And during her time as director of Bonhams auction house, she purchased a rare Elvis Presley collection containing many of his personal items.

It is accurate to say that her behaviour was not in line with the public's perception of an ageing duchess. 'Some people are very surprised,' she told an interviewer, 'but most people are easily surprised, don't you think?' As Deborah rattled on about her love for Elvis, the interviewer seized the opportunity to ask, 'Was he sex on legs?'

'I beg your pardon?' Deborah asked, somewhat baffled.

'Was he sex on legs?' the interviewer nervously repeated.

'I suppose he was,' Deborah answered, thoughtfully repeating, 'I suppose he was.'

DECCA: THE RUNAWAY DEB

Good gracious, she didn't take any clothes to fight in.

– Nanny Blor on Jessica's sudden disappearance

Jessica lived by her own self-inflicted rule: if you feel strongly about something, you ought to go ahead and do something about it. Nancy experimented with the Labour Party, and in the 1930s she and her Oxford friends established a pro-Labour group. When pressed by Jessica to campaign for the party, Nancy laughed it off: 'Oh, darling, you know how it would upset the Poor Old Revereds [their parents] … besides, think of the dreadful boredom …' The complacent attitude of her contemporaries encouraged Jessica to continue on with her socialist fight.

In 1929, at the age of 12, Jessica had opened up her first savings account with Drummonds Bank, a fund which she aptly named her 'Running Away Account'. Throughout the years, Jessica scrimped and saved to build up her account to a sizable amount to live off when the eventful day finally came to run away.

Jessica realised that society was ill divided. She had observed the grim realities of the London slums from the safety of the first-class carriage as the train steamed into London and, as a child, she had accompanied Muv on charitable visits to the poor. Although she empathised with the plight of the working classes, she was observing it all from 'within a fortress' and this realisation caused an irrepressible restlessness.

At first, Jessica complained to Muv about the unfairness of society, and even though Muv lent a sympathetic ear, she could not offer a solution and brushed it off. Jessica accused Muv of being 'an enemy of the working-classes'. Muv was genuinely angered by this accusation for she always treated people as equals and this, she felt, was a step too far: 'I'm *not* an enemy

of the working-class! I think some of them are perfectly sweet!'
Oh yes, Jessica thought, 'perfectly sweet' mental images of
nannies wearing their navy bonnets and butlers in their smart
suits sprung to mind, not the graphic images of suffering and
brutality she was trying to convey.

At the age of 14, Jessica read *Cry Havoc*, the best-selling novel
based on pacifist ideologies, which led her to explore other left-
wing publications, and through self-knowledge she began to
think and feel outside of the confines of her station in life. The
penny had dropped: she could contribute to society, and the
stirrings of a future muckraker were beginning to manifest. It
seemed the Running Away Account might be useful after all.

Years later, when questioned on what attracted her to
communism, Jessica answered: 'That's a perennial question.
I wasn't ever able to answer it in books. Perhaps I should have
to go through psychoanalysis to figure it out.'

Nobody considered Jessica's ideology to be serious. In 1937,
Jessica met her second cousin, Esmond Romilly, at their
mutual cousin's country house, and over the weekend the
rebellious teenagers hatched a plan to escape. Esmond was
leaving for Spain to report on their fight against fascism, and
Jessica had persuaded him to let her tag along. Her enthusiasm
for communism and her healthy bank account convinced him
that she would make an ideal travelling companion. Jessica
and Esmond set about planning her escape. And, ever the
opportunist, before running away, Esmond suggested that
it would be a good idea if they purchased a camera for their
travels. Jessica visited the Army and Navy Stores and charged
an expensive camera to Farve's account.

Esmond was the brains behind their running away
scheme and suggested that Jessica should forge a letter.
She remembered her wealthy friends, the Paget twins, who
travelled extensively during the summer months. With a fool-
proof story, Esmond penned the infamous letter. 'Darling

Decca', the forged letter began, in which the 'Paget twins' frivolously chatted about their motoring trip around Austria en route to Dieppe, where they had hoped Jessica would be permitted to join them at their summer house.

Muv, completely deceived by the chatty letter, thought Jessica's invitation to Dieppe was a most generous offer and granted her permission to travel there ahead of the world cruise which she had arranged as a treat for her youngest daughters to. She also gave Jessica a £30 advance on her cruise wardrobe, which Jessica stashed away for their living expenses in Spain. It was onward and upward from there.

JESSICA'S GUIDE TO RUNNING AWAY

Never tell a living soul and never put anything in writing.

– Jessica

- 📰 Open a bank account as soon as possible.
- 📰 Save all money and sell unwanted things to supplement your income.
- 📰 Be honest about the Running Away Account for when the time comes your parents won't suspect a thing.
- 📰 By the time everyone realises you are gone, you will be halfway across the Continent.
- 📰 Learn casual phrases in French and Spanish. This will make travelling much more flexible.
- 📰 Hatch a fool-proof plan. Forge a letter in the disguise of an invitation to join friends abroad, post the letter from the nearest town and act inquisitive when the letter arrives.
- 📰 Drop casual phrases beforehand, such as, 'Oh how lovely it would be to get away from it all' or 'How one longs for a holiday, do admit'.

- Pretend to be indifferent about the 'invitation' as this will only provoke encouragement from the others that you should accept. Reluctantly agree.
- Pack a small selection of clothing, but leave enough behind to suggest that you are coming back from your 'holiday'.
- Have a partner in crime who is as eager to run away as you are. This should quell any last-minute doubts or nerves.
- Arrange for your partner to meet you on the train, bus or aeroplane. Don't blow your cover by meeting openly in view of the others before you step on to the transport.
- Send chatty postcards or letters about your trip.
- Eventually be honest that you have, in fact, run away and that you are not returning home. It's not nice to make the loved ones fret.
- Be prepared for all hell to break loose.
- Most importantly, be prepared to suffer the consequences.

The Aftermath

Jessica has only taken two pairs of knickers and they are both too small and I'm afraid they will burst.

– Nanny Blor on Jessica's unsuitable
running away clothes

When the news of Jessica's elopement to Spain reached England just about everyone had an opinion on the matter. Several aunts and cousins felt Jessica should be allowed to legally marry Esmond and then divorce him as it would secure her an allowance and a flat where she could live out her days as a social outcast.

Even Hitler had an opinion on the elopement when Unity told him, 'My sister Decca has run away to Spain with the reds';

he apparently sank his head into his hands and sighed, '*Armes Kind*' ('poor child').

Deborah walked around in a cloud of gloom, singing made-up words to the hit song *Somebody Stole My Gal*: 'Somebody stole my Hon, somebody stole my Hon, someone came and took her away, she didn't even say that she was leavin'.'

Meanwhile, the newspapers were having a field day with stories of 'Red Decca'. Unity was frightfully jealous that Jessica was the first one in the family to have her face featured on posters.

Nancy and Peter Rodd devised a plan to telegram Jessica, who was living in Bermeo, northern Spain, to inform her that they were travelling over on a British destroyer and could she possibly meet them at the port. Although suspicious of Nancy's intentions, Jessica travelled 30 miles to meet her, but after waiting for an hour she was nowhere to be found. An English captain approached Jessica to inform her that Nancy had a change of heart and would she kindly step on board for a spot of luncheon. The thought of food appealed to Jessica but she insisted she could not go on board for she knew something was afoot. Nancy later confessed the food had been a ploy to get Jessica on the ship, the next step was locking her in a room and delivering her home to England.

NANCY'S TEASE

Sisters stand between one and life's cruel circumstances.

– Nancy to Jessica

Sisters were life's cruel circumstance.

– Jessica to Nancy

Nancy had special teases for each sibling which she distributed when they least expected it. She began with her youngest sisters and highlighted the unflattering sounds pronounced by the middle syllables of their names: 'U-*nit*-y, Jes-*sick*-a and De-*bor*-ah.'

No one failed to notice the rapid rate at which Unity was growing. By the age of 12 she was so large that Muv complained, 'Oh dear, poor Boud, she is rather enormous.' Nancy had a cruel, rather to-the-point description for her: 'Hideous.'

Nancy would encourage the other siblings to form a circle around Deborah and they would chant: 'Who's the least important person in this room? *You!*' And when Deborah was taken up to bed, Nancy would snide: 'As soon as you're gone I shall do the joy dance.' As Deborah lay in bed, she could hear Nancy jumping up and down, clapping her hands.

Childhood is a hateful age – no trailing clouds of glory – and children are generally either prigs or gangsters and always dull and generally ugly.

– Nancy

When the children were getting on her nerves, Nancy would snap, 'Run along up to the schoolroom we've all had quite enough of you.' Diana had a phobia of being sent away to boarding school and Nancy would play on her fears by sauntering into the room and casually saying, 'Last night after you had gone to bed I was talking you over with Muv and Farve, we were saying how good it would be for you to go to school.'

Nancy preyed on Pamela's weaknesses and made her the basis of all jokes. During the 1926 General Strike, Nancy took the opportunity to turn a national emergency into a joke when she dressed up as a tramp to frighten Pamela, who was running a canteen for strike-breaking lorry drivers. Nancy crept into the quiet canteen, and as Pamela stood behind the counter awaiting her first customer, she sallied forth and grimly pressed her filthy face against Pamela's cheek and barked, 'A cup o' tea miss.' As Pamela nervously poured the tea, Nancy crept behind the counter and grabbed her by the waist. 'How's about a kiss?' she advanced. Pamela lost her balance, fell backwards and almost broke her leg.

2

Looking the Part

The Perils of Pennies

One must never be deterred from doing what one wants for lack of money.

– Nancy

As any U person knows, there is no shame in being a spendthrift. It is the careless and nouvelle riche who lavishly throw their money around. Farve, although a lord, had little money of his own, and the family had to survive on a budget to make the money stretch.

The Mitfords were by no means a poor family in comparison to the very poor of that era, but living in a large house, keeping many animals and with an ever-growing family, it was inevitable that every penny counted. Muv raised hens and sold their eggs to restaurants in London to pay the governess' salary, and Deborah came up with an ingenious plan to sell her hens' eggs to Muv, who agreed to the arrangement and offered Deborah a small payment. This not only benefited Deborah financially, but it also taught her the perils of money management, a field in which Muv was a professional, and whose traits Pamela inherited. Jessica remembered that keeping hens and selling eggs was 'the mainstay' of their personal economy.

Goldie Newport, who knew Pamela during her years at Tullamaine Castle, Co. Tipperary, described her spendthrift ways:

> She [Pamela] also always carried a square basket on her arm. She used to bring eggs to town and sell them to one or two shops. My mother admired the basket one day and Mrs. Jackson said, 'It is rather lovely, isn't it? The German prisoners of war made it, the poor darlings.' Her gardener, Ted Young, used to sell us a beautiful box of mixed vegetables every week. I don't know how my mother got that privilege. It was the first time we were introduced to purple sprouting broccoli and it came from Mrs. Jackson's vast kitchen garden in Tullamaine. She always won prizes for her flowers and vegetables at the local shows. Mrs. Jackson once said to my mother when buying ice-cream in our shop, 'I can buy it cheaper in Cahir,' and my mother said, 'Then that's the place to buy it, Mrs. Jackson.'

Muv meticulously worked out the cost of washing and ironing an average of nine table napkins, for each of the three meals a day, 365 days a year, and found it to be a staggering sum, and as a result she eliminated napkins from the dining room table. 'Paper ones would of course, have been unthinkable, and individual napkin rings too disgusting for words,' Jessica said. So the family just did without, and because it was such an extraordinary thing to do at the time, the *Daily Express* leapt on to the titbit and ran the headline: 'Penny Pinching Peeress.'

Following her discovery of how to save money through cutting back on unnecessary expenses, Muv hoped to pass her economical knowledge on to her children when she challenged them to make up a budget for a young couple living on £500 a year. The child with the most efficient budget would receive half a crown as a reward. Nancy scoffed and hastily scribbled, 'Flowers … £490.00', leaving £10 for other necessary expenses, which, naturally, ruined the competition.

Years later, and well into her middle age, Nancy could be financially savvy when it suited her. To save on the cost of purchasing expensive reading glasses, Nancy chose a pair of glasses provided by the National Health Service: 'My specs are lovely and I had a choice of six different rims so I chose blonde tortoiseshell. I can't see why anybody should mind, it must be pure jealously. And they have a case (specs do I mean).'

SELF SUFFICIENCY

I must earn money when I can – I shall never inherit any as far as I know, haven't got any except what I make, and extreme old age looms all too near.

– Nancy

Throughout their adult lives, each of the girls experienced the ebb and flow of personal finances and they knew how to get the best value out of their trivial investments. Nancy often lived off her wits, writing chatty articles which paid enough to cover her London living expenses. However, she frequently borrowed money from Diana or she headed back to Swinbrook with a heavy heart to write a novel, and when she got paid an advance the London lifestyle would begin again.

In the early days of her marriage to Peter Rodd, Nancy lived off her bridge winnings. She would set up a small card school in her tiny kitchen, invite a few friends over and gamble for housekeep money.

Strapped for cash and possessing a talent to exploit, Jessica and Esmond, at the height of their elopement scandal, decided to sell an interview through their friend, Peter Neville, to the *News Chronicle*, with a plan to pocket the profits.

On a similar theme, the *Daily Express* ran an article on Jessica's elopement and through shoddy reporting had mistakenly used Deborah's name and photograph. Deborah sued the newspaper for libel and was awarded a settlement of £1,000 out of court on the grounds that her position in the marriage market had been threatened.

Perhaps Jessica was the first sister to discover her talent at making money from the simplest things. At the age of 12, Jessica had her appendix removed and sold one of the five stitches to Deborah for 6*d*, and then she auctioned off her appendix, preserved in a jar of methylated spirits, for £1. She sent the other four stitches on as gifts to Diana and a friend.

Earlier still, at the age of 9, Jessica had discovered the joy of sending off for free samples of food. She was particularly fond of Benger's baby food: 'It tasted like Horlicks.' Jessica 'let her imagination rip' and she went to great lengths to describe, in gory detail, the phantom afflictions that plagued her imaginary babies. The arrival of their postman, laden down with free samples, was the highlight of their otherwise dreary day.

FASHION & FINANCES

There were so many of us that even my clothes were not my own, I was just their tenant.

– Diana

As children, the Mitfords seldom went shopping for clothes and they rarely owned anything that was brand new. Their wardrobe consisted of hand-me-down skirts and rough, threadbare jerseys. They had a smart coat for church and special outings, and only received a dress allowance when seasonal travelling clothes were required. Diana's sister-in-law from her first marriage, Grania Guinness, was the same age as Deborah, but taller, and would send over her cast-off clothing from the smart children's retailer Wendy.

When Nancy became a best-selling author with *The Pursuit of Love*, her finances changed forever, and so did her spending habits. Nancy could now afford to purchase custom-made couture dresses and she frequented the showrooms of Balmain, Dior and Lanvin to view their seasonal collections. She spared no expense with her clothes but she still had an eye for a bargain and was not above haggling with the Parisian fashion houses.

Deborah also owned a lot of couture, and being a fan of Dior, she would head straight to the fashion house as soon as she stepped foot in Paris. On one particular trip, her studious daughter, Lady Emma, wanted to visit inside Notre Dame, to which Deborah impatiently said, 'You've seen the outside, now imagine the inside, let's go to Dior.'

In their youth, the girls were also well acquainted with the virtues of swapping and borrowing clothes. Their maid ran up evening dresses for £1 at a time, often copying popular haute couture styles from *Vogue*, which Nancy would later have a penchant for. They also shared a dress known as 'The Wonder Gown' between them, especially Diana and Unity. Unity, being larger than Diana, had the dress let out and then passed it on to Diana as maternity wear when she was expecting a baby. Jessica once advised Deborah to turn an unwanted chiffon dress into a chic evening blouse.

Deborah's rich friend, Bunny Mellon, ordered from Balenciaga's couture collection three times a year and used to send her unwanted designer clothes over to Deborah's mother-in-law for her charity collection. Nancy and Diana would secretly take first pick of what they wanted of the 'mercy parcels' and cunningly replace the Balenciaga with their own well-worn cast-offs. They were caught red handed when Bunny spied Diana wearing her custom-made Dior coat, the only one of its kind in the world. A cautionary tale, indeed!

In 1941, Deborah longed for a lavish wedding dress but did not have the ration coupons to pay for an expensive gown, so she recruited Nancy into finding out from Cecil Beaton who would be the best theatrical costumer to make the dress. Deborah's gown was made by Victor Steibel, who used tulle and chiffon to create the voluminous gown. The savings allowed Deborah to splash out on her unmentionables, which, of course, shall remain unmentionable.

Establishing a Uniform

Oh dear, I do wish she were a little tidier I must say because then she would be perfection – I do feel it's a duty for people like her to be a little bit elegant.

– Nancy on Deborah's country casuals

The Mitfords knew that the key to looking effortlessly smart every day was down to establishing a uniform. We must rule Nancy out of this practice for she spent her days, as a celebrated author, wearing ankle-length Dior dresses. I am mainly referring to Pamela, Diana and Deborah's everyday look.

It's terrible to love clothes as much as I do and perfectly inexplicable because I'm not vain at all.

– Nancy

PAMELA

Pamela wore a thick knitted jumper, usually of Aran wool, with a heavy cardigan and a quilted jacket over the top. She was renowned for her heavy cardigans. Sensible shoes were worn, always, especially in old age when her right leg, which had been inflicted with childhood polio, had become increasingly lame. When Pamela's tweed skirts or heavy cardigans were no longer useful, she passed them on to her dogs to use as bedding. Goldie Newport described Pamela's everyday look:

> She had pale skin, short blonde hair, which was straight and hung over one eye sometimes – Veronica Lake style! She had the most astonishing blue eyes. She seemed to live in a navy three-quarter length coat with brass buttons, a grey skirt and flat laced shoes-all very sensible but stylish, like herself really. In summer she wore a lighter and flared skirt-linen or cotton, I suppose, of pale blue mostly, to match her eyes, and the most beautiful blouses I had ever seen and flat sandals. She never went in for fashion but she always looked lovely and really simply classic. I don't ever remember seeing any jewellery of any kind not even a brooch or engagement ring.

DIANA

Unless one can afford the grandees there is literally nothing on the clothes front.

— Diana

Diana was fond of lightweight, cashmere knits, the waists of which were always cinched by a chic belt. She would accessorise with statement earrings and a string of pearls.

Ballet flats never looked frumpy with her mid-length skirts because she was 5ft 10in tall. Although in her later years she was never materialistic where fashion was concerned, she did appreciate fine tailoring and sharp lines which emphasised her svelte, unchanging figure.

Givenchy had a boutique. I never bought clothes from what they call upstairs which was the expensive part. But in the boutique you could choose something and they'd give you a fitting or even two. You know I still wear them, they haven't dated at all. If I put on something Hubert has made I always feel in the height of fashion.

— Diana

In her late eighties, Diana moved from Orsay to Paris, and settled into a spacious flat on the *Rue de l'Université*, known as the Mayfair of Paris. Diana lived close to the offices of French *Vogue* and often passed the building on her daily walks, where the young fashion editors would rush to the window to catch a glimpse as she passed in her 1950s Balenciaga and Dior suits. She was unaware of the girls pressing their faces against the glass to watch this elegant, elderly lady. To the girls in the office, she had become a fashion icon.

UNITY

Oh dear, poor Boud, she is rather enormous.
— Muv on Unity's stature

Unity adopted the British Union of Fascists' trademark black shirt as her everyday uniform. And during her Germany years she often emulated Diana's simple style of wearing a jumper with a Peter Pan collar, wool skirt and swastika pin.

JESSICA

Clothes were merely coverings to keep her warm; colours and shapes were thrown together hugger-mugger and made you wonder at her choice.
— Deborah on Jessica's wardrobe

Jessica cared little about fashion or what she wore on a daily basis, and she suffered criticism from her nearest and dearest as a result of her careless attitude towards clothing. Much to Nancy's amusement, she befriended Jessica's mother-in-law, Aranka, who made annual visits to Paris to buy inventory for her hat shop in New York City. Aranka bemoaned Jessica's appearance, a titbit which Nancy eagerly shared with her sisters. Endless shrieks prevailed.

'Why can't she dress like you? Why is she such a slattern?' Aranka complained. Nancy divulged more information regarding Jessica and Bob's casual clothing: 'My Bob used to be so smart he was called The Duke. I wish you could see him now – terrible.' Nancy gleefully absorbed the insults and, to conclude Aranka's dismay, she confided to Nancy that when she first met Jessica she 'cried for a week, so dirty'.

Jessica nonchalantly replied, 'Well, Aranka, next time you see her [Nancy], tell her I'm dressed by J.C. Penny.'

DEBORAH

She was pale, with no make-up, beautiful and melancholy-merry.

– James Lees-Milne on Deborah

Deborah labelled her everyday outfit 'My school mistress uniform' because of its sensible appearance: a crisp shirt with collar turned up, of course, usually livened up with contrasting cuffs. The colour was mainly blue, which matched her eyes so perfectly, or pink – a colour advised by Nancy because 'it blues the eyes'. The shirt was always tucked in for a pristine appearance. Deborah completed this outfit of choice with a string of pearls adorned with a diamond clasp, a Devonshire family heirloom, which became her jewellery staple.

—⁊⁊⁊—

DEBORAH'S FASHION ADVICE

In England if you are a duchess you don't need to be well dressed—it would be thought quite eccentric.

– Nancy

- Buy 'stout' clothes from agricultural shows. They will outlive you.
- Avoid the Knightsbridge shops and the garish clothes that are sold in them.
- Marks & Spencer should be an option when one needs something less expensive and more wearable.
- After the above venue has been consulted, one should head to Paris for their bits and bobs. 'Nothing in between seems to be much good.'

The epitome of English aristocracy, the Duchess of Devonshire, feeding her chickens in pearls and wellingtons.

– Luella Bartley

Have you noticed that none of the girls, except for Jessica, ever wore trousers in their everyday life? 'TROUSERS!' Nancy shrieked. 'Well if she goes to Russia in them she'll be lynched, because no women wear them, not even the poor devils who mend the roads.' The girls only wore trousers for hunting, shooting and fishing. It was a question of U and Non-U, really.

NANCY ON FASHION

What is very pretty this year are stoles made of cloth and velvet if one can't afford a good fur.

– Nancy's fashion advice, 1948

In 1959, Nancy offended fashion designers all over the British Isles when she stated, 'The English have never learned to make a skirt.' The president of the Incorporated Society of London Fashion Designers, Lady Pamela Berry, retaliated with, 'This just isn't true', and she challenged Nancy to attend London Fashion Week to see the high-quality designs for herself. 'Sorry,' Nancy replied, but she was otherwise engaged that week. She was sunning herself on the Venice Lido.

Without remorse, Nancy justified her statement:

If I had to cut down on clothes, I would get one suit every year from a good Paris dressmaker. It is a myth that English suits and jackets are superior to French ones.

They have never learned to make a skirt. Last time I was in London I saw a suit, the jacket of which delighted me, but the skirt was quite impossible.

Nancy, always an admirer of Parisian fashion, chronicled her love of clothes in various essays and newspaper articles. Here is a step-by-step guide on how to approach fashion from Nancy's point of view.

NANCY'S GUIDE TO FASHION

My old white Dior dress – perfectly lovely. These dresses are worth getting in spite of the awful price.

– Nancy

⌂ When in England, store new dresses away for two years. It is too common to be in the height of fashion. Being in the height of fashion is for starlets and harlots.

⌂ When in England, refrain from wearing sparkling new clothes. The English do not aspire to look brand new. That would be considered bad manners and reflect terribly on one's good breeding.

⌂ Before purchasing new clothes, always turn them inside out to inspect the seams.

Note to reader: Nancy once bought a suit from a reputable London shop and brought it to her Paris dressmaker for some alterations. The dressmaker was so embarrassed by the suit that she took it home with her in the evenings, lest the fellow dressmakers caught a glimpse of the sloppy craftsmanship. She asked Nancy how she could have invested in such a badly made outfit once she noticed the seams; Nancy shamefully admitted that she had not thought of that.

⚱ If one is male, wear one's new suit around the garden for a day or two to make it appear at least a year old.

⚱ If one is a duchess one is not expected to be well dressed, that would be too eccentric.

⚱ Do not wear a skirt with a 'cunning slit' up the back for it will divide the calves horribly.

⚱ Open-toed shoes, in the style of Princess Margaret, are extremely vulgar.

⚱ Trousers are for peasants, the poor devils who mend the roads and those of a dubious sexuality. It should be known that the sight of trousers does fill one with gloom and apprehension and by wearing such a garment one is setting oneself up for a lynching.

⚱ When the climate influences one's choice of clothing, always go with what looks nice and spare little thought to the chilly weather – one can always wear woollen underthings, perish the thought.

⚱ Don't bother with slips or petticoats: French women don't and they are the last word on fashion.

⚱ Never settle for cheaply made imitations. If one cannot afford the real thing, one should focus on something else, such as cooking or an education.

Style, swank, swagger and showing off; indeed it represents everything that the English most dislike.

– Nancy

How to Dress Like a Mitford Girl

A friend in tweed is a friend indeed.

– Deborah

- Ignore clothing fads and fleeting trends.
- Clothes must have character. Do try to avoid anything that looks brand new.
- Knitwear should be thrown over an outfit of choice. Pamela perfected this look.
- Plaid or tweed skirts – usually the skirt that completes one's Saturday suit – should be worn on a weekday.
- A quilted or tweed jacket should be worn when in the countryside. A wool coat should be reserved for trips into town.
- Anything in herringbone will make one reminisce of Swinbrook.
- Lace-up ankle boots, Oxfords or spectator shoes are authentically Mitford.
- A beret or cloche cap, worn on top of a shingled bob, completes a glamorous Mitford look.
- Accessorise with pearls, not elaborate jewels.
- If one insists on wearing trousers, one should aspire to wear jodhpurs.
- Long or short riding boots, as worn by Deborah, add an element of country chic.
- Stately homes can be draughty; one must never forget to layer an outfit over the top of a liberty bodice, preferably lined in fleece.
- Don't appear too polished. One must look effortlessly put together.

One has achieved an authentic Mitford look when one is:
- The spitting image of Lady of the Manor.
- Asked where the local Saturday hunt has gathered.

- Mistaken for a jockey.
- Asked for directions to the pony club.
- Attacked by animal rights groups for looking as though one indulges in blood sports.

———⁓———

THE MITFORD GUIDE TO PRIMPING

Face cream costs less than gym shoes, you know, and a sprig of rosemary in rain water, the foundation of a good complexion, nothing at all.

— Nancy

Deborah often criticised people on how they behaved and not on their looks – a rather admirable quality. People might not be able to help their overall physical look, but there are ways to maintain a tidy appearance. And, as Nancy advised, 'Rest is everything.'

PALE & INTERESTING

In her frivolous youth, Nancy was known to stain her skin with coffee beans. This was very shocking, as it was considered Non-U to deliberately sport an overly tanned complexion, which Nancy called: 'One mass of well-oiled cracks.' The Edwardian ideal of beauty, the era in which Nancy, Pamela and Diana were born into, matched Farve's views of women being at their most attractive when their natural complexion was revealed. Diana recalled: 'We were quite accustomed to make-up being disapproved of; it was a phobia of Farve's, but in those days it was the fashion.'

It is a popular story in the Mitford family circle that Hitler initially refused to meet Diana and Unity on their first trip to Germany due to their excessive make-up. They were 'made up to the eyebrows', and this cosmetically enhanced look went against the Führer's ideals of natural beauty.

Upon wearing a full face of make-up for the first time, Nancy noticed that all women deliberately tried to catch a glimpse of their reflection as they passed any mirrored object, not because of vanity, but to check that everything was as it seemed.

HAIR

All hell broke loose in the family home when Nancy defied Farve's orders and cut off her waist-length hair into a popular style known as the Shingle, which was simply a Marcel waved bob. Muv was beside herself, worrying that Nancy's position in the marriage market had been thwarted due to her sexless hairstyle, and Farve thought it was awfully masculine to have chin-length hair. Ironically, the opposite sex found Nancy more appealing with her Shingled hair.

Nancy had to stop dyeing her greying hair because of an allergic reaction to the black dye, something which displeased her beyond belief. Pamela once dyed her hair orange, and in the words of Deborah, 'She looked like a tart'.

Cecil Beaton described Deborah's low-maintenance hairstyle as a 'farm work hairdo'. And Deborah warned against a dramatic haircut when, in the 1960s, she had her hair cut by a reputable London hairdresser. Not watching what he was doing, Deborah discovered that her new style made her look like a variety of characters, mainly (in her words): a prison wardress, a Great Dane breeder and an active lesbian; in fact, anything but an ordinary English lady.

NAIL POLISH: A RATHER NEW INVENTION AT SWINBROOK ...

In the 1920s, Nancy's friend came to luncheon at Swinbrook with her nails painted a blood-red colour. Farve looked at the girl in question and, with a deadpan expression, he said, 'I am so sorry!' She questioned why and Farve added, 'I am so sorry to see you have been in a bus accident.'

NANCY'S BEAUTY TIPS

Huge fur hats are simply glam.

– Nancy

Every evening, in her middle age, Nancy wore 'Frownies', which were strips of sticky tape applied to the forehead in an attempt to ward off wrinkles.

If one is looking faded, Nancy recommended that one might try a few feminine wiles such as:

- A darker fond de teint.
- A soupçon of hair dye.
- And especially clothes of brighter hue – especially pink which blues the eyes.
- Eschew grey.

DIANA'S TIPS ON STAYING YOUNG

There's something much more important than beauty, and that is charm.

– Diana

Diana discovered, in her early twenties, that excessive smiling and frowning caused wrinkles. For the better part of her dazzling socialite existence in the 1930s she remained tight-lipped and frozen-faced. Diana passed on her words of wisdom to Unity, who had an entirely different reason for maintaining a solemn expression in photographs. For years and years, Unity survived on a quirky diet of mashed potatoes and, as a result of this, her teeth were very bad. Thus, from an early age, Unity put on her 'photography face', which was a rather sullen expression, when put before a camera.

How to Achieve the Photography Face

❧ Expressionless face.
❧ Relaxed mouth.
❧ Blank stare.
❧ Most of all, an indifference to the camera.

3

At Home & Abroad

Although the Mitfords are looked upon as being the utmost example of British eccentricity, they did not permanently live in England. Unity, the first to leave in 1934, relocated to Munich to study art, learn German and to stalk Hitler. She lived abroad until 1940, returning home to England to recuperate after her suicide attempt. Had war not been declared, she probably would have remained in Germany, the place she loved most, forever.

After striking a fortune with the publication of *The Pursuit of Love*, Nancy moved to Paris and remained in France until her death in 1973. A devoted Francophile, Nancy set up home in a spacious apartment on the stylish *Rue Monsieur* and immersed herself in the French culture. Always preferring abroad to England, the reasons for her immigration were:

- The bad food.
- The awful weather.
- The unfashionable clothes.
- The absurd social customs.

What irritated Nancy most about England was the royal family. She deplored King George VI and Queen Elizabeth, and her annoyance filtered down to the little princesses, Elizabeth and Margaret. Throughout her life, Nancy poked fun at their fashion sense, comparing Princess Anne to an Eskimo, and she wondered what Deborah saw in the Queen Mum, whom she lovingly nicknamed 'Cake'.

Social customs never held much esteem for Nancy, who was very much like Jessica in her liberal thinking and lifestyle. She hated rigid conformity and the fiendish side of Nancy's wit meant that she sought opportunities to attack the much-loved royals, using them as a device to start arguments with her royalist relatives and friends, all in the name of entertainment.

In 1949, Diana and Sir Oswald left England to set up home in Ireland. Their notoriety in the press, his ban from speaking on BBC programmes and public disregard heavily influenced their decision to emigrate from England. Ireland proved to be a hub of luxury; low tax and non-rationing lured many Britons there, Pamela and Derek Jackson included.

Diana adored Ireland, and she found the quiet, non-intrusive surroundings to be bliss. 'Oh Ireland, the niceness of it,' she once said. Nobody treated her with contempt and she was free to go about her daily business. From her Irish house, a converted bishop's palace in Co. Galway, she edited manuscripts and articles for Sir Oswald's publishing company, Euphorion Books.

In 1951, the Mosleys moved to France, where they enjoyed a resurrection in their social life. Not treated with scorn and free to attend functions, Diana and Sir Oswald were completely happy and became friends with their equally infamous neighbours, the Duke and Duchess of Windsor.

In the late 1940s, Pamela and Derek moved to Tullamaine Castle in Co. Tipperary, Ireland, to escape the super taxation of the rich. The post-war years saw Pamela, Diana and Deborah as neighbours in Ireland, with Deborah spending holidays at Lismore, the Devonshire family castle, in Co. Waterford.

Nancy boarded the Aer Lingus Friendship plane to Dublin every summer, where she too enjoyed the 'pre-new world atmosphere' of Ireland. Once an Irish man snapped, 'Hell would be a more suitable place for you, Miss Mitford.'

Jessica, on her twenty-first birthday, inherited the princely sum of £100 and immediately purchased one-way tickets to New York for herself and Esmond. They found themselves in an entirely new world, different from anything they had experienced before. Everything about America seemed optimistic to the young couple, and totally alien at the same time.

Everybody loved Jessica and Esmond, and they were welcomed with open arms into New York society. They were young, intelligent, good conversationalists and, most of all, they loved America. They had originally planned to stay in America for the duration of the war and move back to England once it was over. However, after Esmond's death in 1941, Jessica stayed in America and moved to San Fransisco. She settled in Oakland, California, and remained there until her death in 1996.

NANCY ON THE DULLNESS
OF ENGLAND IN SEPTEMBER

Oh, I hope I never live there again.
— Nancy on returning to England

Nancy thought September was the worst time of the year to visit England, and she summarised her thoughts in a few key sentences. In Nancy's words, this is why one should never visit England:

- The long, boring days in the countryside where one simply aches with boredom.
- The trees all go black from the damp and lack of sunlight, unlike the trees in Paris, where the leaves are pretty and green.
- The wasps and biting flies.
- Last but not least, it becomes damp in the garden after tea, which simply ruins one's mood.

AN ENGLISHWOMAN IN PARIS

Oh, my passion for the French. I see all through rose coloured spectacles!

– Nancy

In 1966, the *London Sunday Times* reported: 'Nancy Mitford has lived for twenty years in Paris, yet when anyone bumps into her in the street they always look at her and say sorry in English.' The article inspired Nancy to make comparisons between her Parisian tastes and her English identity.

Her first comparison was her drawing room, which she thought was typically French in its decor. Nancy confessed that when people came to visit they would glance around and announce, 'What a lovely English room!' Nancy, unnerved by their statement, blamed the pink curtains.

'I just can't help being terribly English. I look English,' she confided. 'There's a skeleton in The Musée de l'Homme in Paris called "English-Woman". I always look at it and think, that's me.'

Muv's Scottish Island

After the war, Muv retired to her private island, Inch Kenneth. The main attraction of the island, for Muv, was the fact that no tourists visited, and the only way to access the island was by boat, providing the sea allowed for a smooth crossing. Her days were long and sometimes lonely, so to pass the time Muv scanned the mainland with her telescope, hoping to catch sight of weary tourists who had pitched a tent. As soon as the tent appeared, she sent the boat out and the tourists were ferried over for an enormous tea.

Jessica's American Life

We lead an extremely un-duchessy life here.
— Jessica to Deborah, 1951

In October 1951, Deborah planned her stateside visit to Jessica. Before the impending visit, Jessica wrote to Deborah to forewarn her of a few domestic things, mainly highlighting the smallness of their suburban home in contrast to the grandeur of Chatsworth. Deborah, now a duchess, would have to (from a lofty point of view) slum it in America. Jessica specifically alerted Deborah's attention to:

❧ The sleeping arrangements: Deborah would have to sleep on a sofa in the dining room because there was no spare bedroom. Deborah could stay in a hotel, but there were some factors standing in her way, mainly the rule that a visitor could not bring more than $25 into America. 'So you will be at our mercy once here,' Jessica warned her.

❧ Daily life was very uncertain for Jessica. Many of her friends were being arrested and she wasn't sure if she would be next. 'Not that we expect to be, but I'm just warning you,' Jessica confided.

❧ Jessica worked day and night for civil rights organisations, but naturally she would take one or two weeks off work to entertain Deborah. However, should an emergency arise, she would have to 'scram' back to work.

❧ Deborah must avoid making a serious error like Muv, who before her visit had cabled Jessica: 'Am considering smuggling some things into US to sell, please suggest best things to bring.' Jessica was convinced the FBI would send customs to raid her house.

Deborah's First Impressions

After receiving Jessica's cautionary tale, Deborah braced herself for the worst, and upon her arrival immediately penned her feelings to Diana, confiding that the entire first impression had caused her 'such a turn'. As soon as she regained her composure, Deborah gathered her thoughts:

❧ Jessica appeared as a stranger to her: she had 'lost all colour, even her eyes look different'. Nonetheless, Deborah quickly concluded that people often physically chang between the ages of 20 and 35.

❧ The hot Californian climate was 'dreadful' and 'airless' and 'must be bad for people'. It certainly wasn't Blighty.

❧ Jessica's American accent startled her the most. Not only had she adopted an American accent, but she also said 'completely American sentences'. When Deborah asked her how old Bob was, she answered, 'Pushing forty'.

Again, Deborah in a state of trauma, added, 'It's the voice I can't get over.'

Needless to say, Deborah checked into a hotel.

—⁓—

The Mitford Guide

To a Shooting Party

✓ As a rule, women are useless at a shooting party. The sooner one has learned this, the better. Nobody likes a long face.

✓ If a woman is asked to a shooting party, she must be certain that the man, whose presence she will be responsible for, is willing to go with her.

✓ Should the gentleman decline the offer, the woman cannot attend alone and will have to invent a tactful excuse. 'Oh, *that* weekend? Oh dear, I am otherwise detained.'

✓ If you can attend, enter the date of the shoot neatly into your engagement book.

✓ So as to avoid a lot of interaction prior to the shoot, arrive late – no earlier than tea – but in time to dress for supper.

✓ The houses are draughty, so it is advisable to wear a coat over your evening dress. Chattering teeth and uncontrollable shivering is not an attractive sight.

✓ At dinner, unless you are familiar with the guests, do tread carefully with the topic of conversation, it might not be helpful to gleefully ask, 'Who here supports Mosley!?'

✓ Remember to retreat to your room to recover from the damage that a heavy dinner inflicts upon the face.

✓ Certain meaningless hobbies become wonderful distractions at a shooting party. Remember to pack your embroidery or that enormous book which you bought but have little interest in reading. 'Work' of any sort will be indispensable.

✓ Be considerate to your hostess and remain in bed until twelve o'clock. No hostess wants to be bothered with her female guests in the morning unless there are some men around to amuse them.

✓ You will be expected to venture out with the guns. In these situations, wear your stoutest tweeds, choosing a neutral colour (so as not to shock the birds), thick-soled shoes and a mackintosh.

✓ Approach the returning men with caution. Should the men smile and chat with ease, it has been a good shoot. Should they ignore you, it has been a bad shoot. It is best to wait until they begin the conversation.

✓ If you should hear, 'Shut up and lie down!' Remember he is addressing the dog and not you.

✓ It may be a consolation to remember that the weekend does not last forever. And when you leave, you will instantly appreciate all you had previously overlooked in your own home.

———≈———

Housekeeping with Pamela

Pamela was dedicated to her frugal habits, which were laughed at throughout her sisters' letters. Her actions were not only thrifty during the dark economic depression of post-war Britain, but also ahead of their time too. Ironically, Pamela's husband was a multi-millionaire, and even after their divorce she was very well off and could afford to live extravagantly, but she chose to pinch pennies where she could.

Pamela's Household Hints & Tips

- Choose an aga to match one's eyes. Pamela ordered one in cornflower blue.
- Buy household goods in bulk.
- Never allow the daily worker to clean the bath; they waste too much water.
- Never waste water. When running the hot water tap and waiting for the water to heat up, always run it into a bucket and keep it handy. Use the buckets of water for the vegetable garden where it will always be welcome.

Little Known Facts & Eccentricities

Woman works in mysterious ways.

– Deborah

In 1939, Pamela was a passenger on the second ever commercial flight to cross the Atlantic.

Upon seeing barrage balloons for the first time, Pamela remarked, 'They are so very beautiful and make a wonderful decoration.'

Pamela preferred her dachshunds over children and dedicated her life to her dogs. She cooked rice, a variety of meat and baked brown bread for them to feast on.

Pamela sent Jessica a singing telegram for her twenty-second birthday.

A journalist asked why Pamela preferred to stay in Switzerland, and she answered that her dogs were old and preferred the Continent. She remained in Switzerland until her dogs died.

1 Diana and her eldest son, Jonathan Guinness, 1929. *(By kind permission of Fiona Guinness)*

2 Diana with Desmond and Penny Guinness. *(By kind permission of Fiona Guinness)*

3 Diana with Lady Redesdale, Oxford, 1954.
(By kind permission of Fiona Guinness)

4 Diana leaving Sir Harold
Gillie's office following a
post-operative appointment,
1934. *(By kind permission
of Fiona Guinness)*

5 Diana and Tom Mitford with their cousins, Randolph and Diana Churchill,
and friend, Ralph Jarvis in 1927. *(James Lees-Milne papers 1907–97. By kind
permission of Beinecke Rare Book and Manuscript Library, Yale University)*

6 Nancy wearing her beloved Dior, 1956. The inscription reads: 'Such a happy period on your beautiful island.' *(By kind permission of Locanda Cipriani, Venice)*

7 Jonathan Guinness and Pamela with her beloved dachshund, Rignell, 1939. *(By kind permission of Fiona Guinness)*

8 Deborah as a teenager. *(By kind permission of Fiona Guinness)*

9 Jessica with her daughter, Constancia 'Dinky' Romilly. *(By kind permission of Constancia Dinky Romilly and Benjamin Treuhaft)*

10 Jessica and Esmond. *(By kind permission of Constancia Dinky Romilly and Benjamin Treuhaft)*

11 Unity in a pensive mood, note her swastika pin. *(By kind permission of Stephen Kennedy)*

12 Heywood Hill, where Nancy worked from 1941–45. A blue plaque was erected in her honour. *(By kind permission of David G. Lees)*

13 27 Rutland Gate, an imposing townhouse where the girls lived during the social season. *(By kind permission of Sholom and Meems Ellenberg)*

14 Deborah with her chicken, 'The Chairman who rules the roost', 2011. *(By Kind permission of Jim Dixon, PDNPA)*

15 Deborah, 2011. *(By Kind permission of Jim Dixon, PDNPA)*

16 James Lees-Milne, Pamela and Nancy with a ukulele, 1926. *(James Lees-Milne papers 1907–97. By kind permission of Beinecke Rare Book and Manuscript Library, Yale University)*

17 Swinbrook House. *(By kind permission of Debbie Catling)*

18 'The Cloisters' at Asthall Manor. *(By kind permission of Debbie Catling)*

19 Asthall Manor. *(By kind permission of Debbie Catling)*

20 Batsford Park. *(By kind permission of Debbie Catling)*

Pamela introduced the Appenzeller Spitzhauben breed of chicken to Britain from Switzerland, having smuggled the prohibited eggs through customs inside a chocolate box.

Unity introduced Pamela to Hitler, and rather than discussing foreign policies with him, Pamela decided to chat about the delicious new potatoes which had been served for lunch.

Before leaving Tullamaine, Pamela held an estate sale and declared rather loudly, 'NOTHING IS TO LEAVE THIS HOUSE UNTIL IT IS PAID FOR.'

When Diana was in prison, she sent her youngest children and belongings over to Pamela's house. Pamela wrote to Diana to say:

- Diana's clothes had been moth-eaten so she had burnt the lot. She failed to realise how this would upset Diana, because one appreciated old clothes during wartime rationing.
- She made Diana's baby son, aged just 20 months, walk through a field of thistles.
- She ordered Diana's favourite horse, Edna May, to be slaughtered to free up space for crops.
- She euthanised Diana's dog, Grousy.

Pamela had a favourite description to describe anything wondair: 'Just like the little dog herself,' which was derived from her deep love for her dachshund.

Pamela was famous for her sagas. Nancy described her sagas to be 'Like modern art and literature: pointless and plotless'.

PAMELA'S PETS

'Their names are fantastic and so is their behaviour,' Deborah said of Pamela's dogs. Indeed, Pamela was devoted to her pets. She cooked for them 'all the crank stuff': rice, meat of all kinds and brown bread. Her daily ritual consisted of waking up early, feeding her dogs and then exercising them, much to the dismay of her house guests as the dogs' howls could 'wake the dead'. Those three operations were repeated in quick succession throughout the day.

After a brisk walk through the countryside, Pamela would return home with her dogs. And enforcing no discipline on them, they would come in covered in mud and jump on the sofas. Pamela made no attempt to move them – a sore point with whoever she was staying with. Instead of pushing them off the furniture, she would stop whatever she was doing and talk very loudly to the dogs. The dogs ignored her, of course.

Pamela's pets were very much part of the family and she never treated an animal any less than she would treat a human. In the 1940s, Pamela and Derek loaded their car to set off for a weekend trip to Paris. They had made reservations at the Ritz and booked tickets for the opera. As they were about to set off, Derek noticed their little dachshund in the backseat. They could not bear to hurt the dog's feelings, so they drove to London with the dog and made reservations at Claridges.

———

Pamela's Guide to Throwing a Jubilee Party

- Invite everyone from the town. Of course, they will say no, but rest assured they will come.
- Convert one's barn and decorate it for the occasion with bunting and balloons.
- Alternatively, to save money one can hang tea towels as a substitute for bunting.
- A barbecue is best for dealing with a large group of hungry guests.
- Put on a spread of the best food one can get one's hands on, or afford.
- Serve up sausages, bread rolls and cheddar cheese, eggs pickled and a barrel of beer. Pamela ordered sausages from the local monks and rolls from the nudist colony.
- Co-ordinate games such as: three-legged races, egg & spoon and sack races.
- Light a small bonfire for ambiance.
- Gather around the bonfire to sing the National Anthem.
- Afterwards, write and inform anyone who failed to attend that the party was a stellar success. Do mention they weren't missed as there were *so* many people there.

Mitford Mess

Chop potatoes and tomatoes.
Heat up a saucepan of oil until sizzling.
Carefully add the potatoes and tomatoes to the oil.
Fry until golden brown.
Consume immediately.

CHILDHOOD HOMES

Batsford Park to *Asthall Manor* to *Swinbrook House*.

– Nancy's description of the family's declining fortune

BATSFORD PARK

In 1917, the family relocated from London to Batsford Park, in Gloucestershire. Farve's elderly parents, the previous Lord and Lady Redesdale, were the only occupants of the sprawling house, and the huge rooms had been closed off for years with dust covers strewn over the grand furniture. Wartime restrictions and lack of money did little to alter the state of the house when the family moved in.

The Redesdale estate was valued at £33,000, and after tax and other bequests were made, the fortune came in at just under £17,000 (around £600,000 in today's money). The bulk of the fortune was tied to land in Gloucestershire, Oxfordshire and Northumberland, and the inheritance, what there was in cash, was insufficient to run Batsford. It was obvious that the house would have to be sold, but this would have to wait until after the war.

Nancy, who was 13 at time, found her grandfather's vast library at Batsford to be a source of comfort and endless entertainment. Pamela, who had just recovered from a serious bout of childhood polio and paralysis, settled into the countryside, a place where she would always feel at home. Diana remembered their genteel poverty despite their father's title, and recalled the scratchy fabric of Farve's army coats which Muv had made into winter coats for the children. Unity was a toddler when they moved and Jessica would be born that same year.

It was at Batsford that Muv began her lifelong habit of keeping hens, and she employed a keeper to handle the 500 hens, whose eggs she sold to local shops and then on to smart restaurants in London. The hens' eggs provided a sufficient enough income to pay the governess' yearly salary of £150. Despite Muv's entrepreneurial skills, money would always be tight and the family patiently waited for the end of the war so they could sell the house, hoping the cash would ease their financial troubles.

ASTHALL MANOR

In 1919, Farve sold Batsford Park and looked for a modest property in Swinbrook, a small village in Oxfordshire where he owned land, spacious enough to house his expanding family. The search was fruitless and he settled for Asthall Manor in the neighbouring village. He set about turning it into a family home for his six children, the seventh on its way. The years spent at Asthall were the happiest, and the sale of Batsford gave the Mitford family a fleeting sense of financial security. Farve converted the barn into four bedrooms and constructed a covered passage, 'The Cloisters', to attach it on to the main part of the house. In 1920, Deborah was born and the family was now complete.

A darker element was beginning to stir at Asthall, which would leave a marked impression on Farve, Pamela and Diana. The other children and Muv claimed to have never been troubled by the poltergeist, whose nightly antics did little to discourage them from staying in the house. But Farve, in particular, was troubled by its presence. The poltergeist was said to have torn off the cook's bedclothes in the middle of the night. Farve never quite took to the house in the same way his family did, and relatives believed the haunting was the main reason for its sale in 1926.

SWINBROOK HOUSE

Farve dreamed of building a family home, and in 1926 he set about enlarging a farmhouse in Swinbrook village. While the house was being finished, 'Builder Redesdale' uprooted his family to a cheap hotel in Paris. Farve took his car and he often got into trouble with the French police for driving on the wrong side of the road. When stopped by the police, Farve would wind down his window and shout, 'Sorrry, no Frrrrench', in an exaggerated accent (to make it easier for the policeman to understand).

A few months later, the family returned home and moved into the newly renovated house. The family's reaction was not what Farve had anticipated. 'We all thought the house monstrous,' Diana recalled, and his spirits were crushed when Nancy and Diana renamed it 'Swinebrook'. 'The knives and forks are so cold we can't eat with them,' began their daily, trivial complaints. And Jessica remembered the building had aspects of a medieval fortress prison. Muv, who had an eye for interior design, tried in vain to make the house as lovely as possible but despite her best efforts Nancy still found fault. The doors were made of elm, which is prone to warping, but Farve declared it was 'damn good wood'.

By 1936, Farve's finances were beyond reconciliation and he was forced to sell the house. Deborah described the sale of Swinbrook as the worst thing to happen in her life: 'Nothing has saddened me like the going from Swinbrook.' Farve tried to scale back some money by selling the family's furniture and antiques at one of his many furniture sales, but to no avail. The family, what was left of it, relocated to Old Mill Cottage in High Wycombe.

Rutland Gate

When Asthall Manor was sold, Farve bought the lease on 26 Rutland Gate. The house, located in affluent Knightsbridge, was seven storeys high and stood alone. The house had nine indoor staff that came from Swinbrook House, a ballroom, a drawing room and enough bedrooms for the entire family, though Jessica and Deborah preferred to share. The family also owned the Mews, a tiny flat, once the chauffeur's living quarters, at the back of the house.

The dining room was decorated in the newly fashionable stipple, the only time Muv followed trends. Muv also decorated the large drawing room in grey with gilding and furnished it with the Redesdale French furniture from Batsford.

There was a 'wonderfully unhygienic' communication system between each floor, and to work it one had to blow down the mouthpiece with 'an alarming puff' that made the connecting device on the other floor 'fly out with a whistle'. You could also press your ear to the mouthpiece and hear the caller talking from the other floor. Farve installed a passenger lift, of which, Jessica wrote, 'He was immensely proud'.

An 'odd man', Mr Dryer, lived in the basement and tended to the boiler. At night he slept next to the boiler and never complained of his subterranean existence. Deborah noticed that he never ventured upstairs or to other parts of the house.

When it was time for one of the girls to come out, the family would prepare in advance for their trip to Rutland Gate. Jessica compared their going up to Rutland Gate as 'the evacuation of a small army'. For days, the grown-ups prepared the visit, and mountains of luggage and an endless supply of homemade bread were sent up to the house. For the duration of the season, they would host parties there, and it was here that the girls resided until the season was over. The family would then let the house and retreat back to the countryside.

THE PERFECT GUEST

I'm not much trouble – no meals or hardly just sometimes a little ironing.

— Nancy

Nancy knew how to sell herself as the perfect house guest. She began with a list of pros, followed by a brief list of cons, and was not above exaggerating where necessary. In the style of Nancy, be sure to emphasise that it is the company you are keen to see (this may be a lie) and not the free room (again, a lie).

In the words of Nancy, her personal qualities were as follows:

Pros
- Cheerful.
- Willing to make one's own bed and help clean up.
- Keen to please.
- Can scramble eggs.
- Makes a good cup of tea.

Cons
- Highlight your lack of skills, i.e. cooking elaborate meals.
- Redeem the previous statement by adding: 'Can peel potatoes.'
- When irritated by poor hospitality, you may be liable to offend the host by being overly praiseworthy of anywhere but the actual place you are staying.
- Falls asleep during intervals of boredom.
- Must be entertained endlessly.

PASSPORT PATROL

Following their release from prison, Diana and Sir Oswald's passports were revoked by the Labour government and for two years they applied for them, but to no avail. Unwilling to accept defeat, Sir Oswald discovered in the Magna Carta that there was nothing to stop anyone from leaving England. Passports were only required, by law, to enter a country. Sir Oswald wasted no time in contacting General Franco, who said the Mosleys were welcome to land in Spain, with or without a passport.

Sir Oswald bought a 60-ton yacht, *Alianora*, and the family prepared their travelling arrangements. The Labour government realised that they were going to look foolish and consequently granted them passports.

Jessica did not own a passport and, to hurry the application process along, she became a naturalised American citizen. She was observed by the FBI for her 'un-American activities', and in 1955 the State accidentally issued her a passport. She recalled:

In 1955, the state department issued a passport by mistake and sent a telegram saying: 'Passport issued by mistake. Do not use under penalty of the law.' So we fled, using it every inch of the way, and came back to England for the first time. Now, this was in the very height of what is loosely known as the McCarthy era in America, you know, the witch hunting committees rising high, and all that, and in fact, it really was, you know, a sort of frightening period.

TIPS ON TRIPS

Nancy: All tourists half expect to be murdered, so it is brave, as well as energetic, of them to tour.

Pamela: The motor car is the best way to explore Europe.

Diana: A good holiday must make one feel at least thirty years younger.

Unity: Do not get arrested on a short city break. While visiting Prague, Unity blatantly walked around the city, flaunting her swastika badge. She was arrested and released several hours later, but her passport and Nazi paraphernalia were detained for a further forty-eight hours. How inconvenient!

Jessica: Stay away from nature. It might be helpful to recall Jessica's mantra: 'Nature, nature, how I hate you.' This should be pronounced as 'Nate-cha, Nate-cha, how I hate ya'.

Deborah: Africa is perfectly fascinating once you get there.

NANCY'S TIPS FOR HOLIDAYING IN WINTER

- If one is under 40, please ignore all advice.
- Winter in Europe for those over 40 can be very trying. To prepare oneself for the cold snap, once must carry out certain steps in precise order:
  1. It is best to hire a hotel with a tiny room so one can keep warm in a box-like atmosphere.
  2. Do maintain a room temperature of over eighty.
  3. Seldom leave the room.

4

The Trivialities of Life

Nancy and the War Effort

In 1958, Nancy was invited on to the BBC radio programme *These Foolish Things*, where she, along with a panel of distinguished guests, reminisced about Big Ben and the personal sentimentality it represented. The broadcast had a somber tone, and the guests spoke with great pride and patriotism. When it was Nancy's turn to be interviewed, her voice lilted over the broadcast, in the same tone which had been perfected during the Bright Young Things parties, when the young people had learned how to speak in a high pitch in order to be heard over the loud gramophone records. Nancy decided that Big Ben reminded her of the war, and she remembered her maid, Gladys, who 'absolutely loved' air raids: 'there was nothing she liked better in the world.' After a two-year break from air raids, a large bomb had exploded in the middle of the night and Nancy was 'sitting up in bed, rather sort of wondering', when Gladys put her head around the bedroom door and announced, 'Isn't it a treat to hear them again!'

At the height of the London bombings, Nancy was living on Blomfield Road, Maida Vale, one of the worst hit areas during the Blitz. The nightly air raids made living there impossible and she relocated to Rutland Gate.

The spacious house was being used, rather ironically given Unity's ideology, to shelter Jewish immigrants from Poland who had been evacuated from the East End. It was one of the few times in her life that Nancy felt humbled by other people's bravery, and she did all she could to cheer them up and make their hopeless experience a pleasant one. Behind her hardened shell of wit and teasing, Nancy could be extremely kind.

She tactfully researched the Feast of Esther before purchasing Christmas presents and went to great lengths to organise a dance at the house. Muv was horrified and complained to Nancy that the situation was impossible, with only one maid to clean up the mess. Nancy was undeterred and cheerfully settled into her wartime role.

However, it was not long before Nancy began to see the comic side to the situation. A Jewish girl, aged 16, confided to Nancy that she was pregnant and, being unmarried, this left the girl in a sensitive predicament. Nancy pondered the situation and decided that a very hot bath, followed by a strenuous walk, ought to remedy the problem, but 'anxious that it might not work', she cheerfully said, 'Shall I be obliged to wield a knitting needle and go down to fame as Mrs. Rodd the abortionist?'

In 1941, an intriguing offer presented itself to Nancy. Her friend at the War Office asked her to work at the French Officers' Club as a 'glamorous lady spy'. Nancy was attracted by the idea and explained to the Mitford family friend Mrs Violet Hammersley that her role was, 'To try to find something out about them. They are all here under assumed names, all splashing mysteriously large sums of money about and our people can't find out a thing about them and are getting very worried.'

Nancy found a new life of glamour and excitement at the French Officers' Club. The Free French officers admired her prettiness, her intelligence and her chic style of dressing in sharp tailored clothing to emphasise her slim frame. And before long, Nancy fell in love.

Months earlier, Peter had begun his own affair with Nancy's cousin, which more or less severed whatever cordial arrangement their seven-year marriage had become. As a consequence, when the opportunity presented itself, Nancy felt no guilt in forging a love life of her own outside of marriage, and fell helplessly in love with a Free French officer named André Roy.

André was everything Peter was not: sophisticated, kind and amusing. The affair resulted in Nancy becoming pregnant – a tricky situation for a wife who was not spending any time with her husband, but she carried on nonetheless in a state of bliss. The affair was short-lived and Nancy suffered from an ectopic pregnancy. After her convalescence, she returned to London in the spring of 1942, and began her job at Heywood Hill's bookshop in Mayfair. Months later, Nancy fell in love again.

Rather like the plot of one of her novels, Nancy's great love of her life, Colonel Gaston Palewski, had met Peter before he had met her. A man of the world and an accomplished diplomat, Gaston was used to dining in the company of smart society. It was during a posting to Ethiopia that he met Peter; both men were involved in the Anglo-French negotiations over the Djibouti-Addis railway. One evening, during supper, Gaston heard from Peter that his wife Nancy lived in London and was most eager to hear news from him. Gaston, who was being posted to London, promised to make an appointment with Nancy to report her husband's news.

In September 1942, Nancy met Gaston in the garden of the Allies Club – a respectable meeting place for exiled French officers. They had a congenial chat about Peter, Ethiopia and France, the latter of which Nancy had great enthusiasm for. On that same night, they both discovered a mutual admiration for one another.

A few days later she invited Gaston over to Blomfield Road for supper. After a charming evening, where they laughed and shared stories, mainly Nancy listening to Gaston's tales of France, he departed at dawn to his rented house across the park at Eaton Terrace. A few hours later, the telephone rang and Nancy answered it. '*Alors, Racontez,*' the voice on the line said. And so their affair began.

The Mitford Guide
to Falling in Love

The Mitfords believed if they concentrated hard enough, it should be easy to make anyone fall in love with them. Should your own telepathic skills fail you, and they just might, here are some musings from the girls on the subject of love. They all, except for Unity, married and suffered their own discourse during their marriages and quest to find true love.

Nancy

In her happier moments, which were brief during her marriage to Peter, Nancy stated: 'Marriage is the most important thing in life and must be kept going at any cost; it should be emphasized on where there is, as well as physical love, a complete conformity of outlook.'

A few months later, Nancy realised how unsuited she and Peter were. Nancy's unhappiness and resentment towards Peter, and anybody who was in a loving relationship, mainly Diana, ignited her jealously, and she snapped: 'I honestly do believe marriage is the most dreadful trap and that human beings must have been mad to invent such a relationship. Nobody except a husband can make one *cry* with rage, or make me cry at all, and now my hankies are *wet all day*.'

In 1939 the Rodds separated, and in 1941 they were more or less living apart. Nancy often approached the subject of divorce but Peter remained vague. He admitted the marriage was over and that he was in love with someone else – 'Peter was always in love with someone else' – but could not bring himself to divorce her. Nancy's frustration was paramount, and Peter's evasive attitude to divorce drove her to despair. They officially separated in 1945 when Nancy left for Paris to start a new life without him, and were divorced, finally, in 1957. They were, however, to remain congenial friends, with Peter staying at Nancy's flat during his trips to Paris.

I am really fond of Peter you know but the whole thing is complicated, and the person I live for is the Col.

– Nancy to Diana, 1948

PAMELA

There was never a dull moment.

– Pamela on her marriage to Derek Jackson

Pamela was more suited to companionship rather than a heady love affair. She refused John Betjeman's advances and suffered the indignity when her fiancé, Oliver 'Togo' Watney, called off their engagement after it had been announced in the newspapers. In 1936, at the age of 29, she married the brilliant scientist Derek Jackson.

Pamela followed Derek across the country and to America in the mid-1930s, when he was travelling on top-secret scientific assignments; she even relocated to Ireland so he could focus his full attention on steeplechasing. Derek had odd habits, such as bursting into violent rages and offering unique advice, which usually began in a rough voice: 'Never go to a public lavatory in London. I always pee in the street. You may be fined a few pounds for committing a nuisance, but in a public lavatory you risk two years in prison because a policeman in plain clothes says you smiled at him.'

Derek's outbursts caused Pamela moments of embarrassment. On one occasion, the back windscreen of his car had been covered in mud, obscuring his view, so he took a jack and hurled it through the glass. Trivialities, such as being placed in the wrong class of carriage, enraged him, and to demonstrate his displeasure he would pull the emergency break. He was often fined for various reasons and got into the odd habit of carrying £100 notes, of which he would demand change. Derek also greeted people of his own sex with a kiss (unfortunately, Farve's reaction to such a continental greeting was never recorded) and he was openly bisexual, as Diana explained in her memoirs, *Loved Ones*:

'Would you say Derek was bisexual?' Diana asked Pamela.
'Oh yes, absolutely. He always said, "I ride under both rules.".,' Pamela responded.

When Pamela was decorating the empty rooms of their marital home, Rignell, Derek told her: 'Make it as much like a hotel room as possible.' Pamela wanted for nothing during her marriage to Derek. She was the second of his six wives, and their marriage lasted the longest. It has been said that she was the only one of his many wives who tolerated his quirks and supported his endeavours. Pamela would quietly sit in the corner of the room, reading or sewing, as Derek worked, and when she grew tired and made for bed, he would say, 'Don't go. Please stay.' He preferred a silent, human presence.

Eventually their marriage ended in divorce. Derek remarried and Pamela departed for Europe with her female companion, Giuditta Tommasi. Jessica started the rumour, which has attached itself to Pamela's legacy, that she was a lesbian. 'My sister has become a you-know-what-bian,' she wrote to Bob. It is highly unlikely that Pamela and Giuditta were anything but good friends. No one in the family had reason to believe she was a lesbian, and with a family as open-minded and controversial as the Mitfords, there would have been no reason to keep it a secret. Years later, Derek and Pamela became good friends and he left her a large fortune in his will.

DIANA

I don't want everybody to fall in love with me you know.

– Diana

When Bryan Guinness met Diana, she was an 18-year-old girl hidden away in the Cotswolds, with no formal schooling, wearing hand-made clothes and, except for her spell in Paris, had never ventured far from her nanny's protective gaze. He thought she was the perfect wife for him: a country girl from a large family, who would share his passion for the countryside and be willing to provide him with many children.

Bryan was immensely rich. His family had made their money in the brewing trade; they were worth millions and owned property all over England and Ireland, as well as various homes on the Continent. Diana was the daughter of a penniless peer, and it did not thrill her parents when she expressed her wish to be married into the Guinness family. Earning one's money in trade, despite how rich it could make one, was still a taboo topic among the old-world aristocrats. Muv, who was very economic, also worried about Diana being in charge of a large fortune.

Bryan did not foresee that his beautiful young wife had set her sights on a glamorous life, and still only 19 and in her first year of marriage, she had become one of London's most celebrated hostesses. So beloved was Diana that Emerald Cunard, the revered American socialite, had predicted she would precede her in becoming one of history's great hostesses.

I very much disliked being told, 'No you're not to lunch or dine with so and so.' I thought, how wonderful to be on one's own and do as one pleased.

– Diana

Bryan was obsessed with Diana, and by the time she was 21 she had given him two sons. Diana began to have silly quarrels with Bryan; she accused him of being too possessive and his devoted attention began to make her feel claustrophobic. He pressured her to have more children and discouraged her busy social life; it had been his dream to settle down in the countryside, surrounded by many children. Diana thought two children was plenty, and she was not fond of the countryside, having just escaped it. Diana reflected on their different attitudes, concluding that Bryan preferred pottery whereas she preferred porcelain.

Diana grew increasingly irritated with Bryan's sentimental nature, his devotion to her, and eventually she fell out of love with him. They continued on as before, spending summer on the Venice Lido, throwing parties at their large London townhouse and retreating to their country manor, Biddesden. They were everyone's favourite couple; their blonde hair and bright blue eyes gave them an angelic appearance, but behind the cold gaze of their portraits on the covers of society magazines lay a dark secret which would shake London society.

'I was in love with him, I was in love with life and to me they were more or less identical,' Diana said of Sir Oswald. Bryan was aware of Diana's affair and he begged her to stop. But Diana wanted a clean break; she separated from Bryan and moved to Eaton Square.

Bryan wrote to her, hoping she would return; in the back of his mind he wondered if Sir Oswald's lack of commitment would force her back to the family home. Diana persevered. 'Are you positive that you love Tom [as Sir Oswald was known] more than me? You say you cannot do without him – but can you do without me?' Bryan pleaded with her.

A short while later, Bryan met Elisabeth Nelson, who became his ideal wife; 'A much better wife for him than I was,' Diana would say, and she gave him nine children. Bryan was completely happy with his new life.

In contrast, Diana was facing an uncertain future as the mistress of London's most notorious philanderer. She loved Sir Oswald and tolerated his affairs, often blaming his strong physical attraction as the cause. Eventually, in 1936, they were married in an unconventional ceremony in Joseph and Magda Goebbels' drawing room, with Hitler and Unity serving as their only witnesses.

Though she declared him the great love of her life, those who were privy to their private life together thought otherwise. Sir Oswald wanted Diana all to himself; gone were the days of never-ending luncheons with friends, and they rarely dined with people other than each other. He still had affairs, and was the strong and dominant one in the marriage in their household he was treated as God; his views and opinions, although deplored by the outside world, were the final word so long as Diana was concerned.

To complicate matters, Sir Oswald disliked Nancy – a feeling which was mutual – and Diana was caught in the middle. He did his best to stop Diana visiting Nancy, especially during her lengthy battle with cancer. Diana would set off 'half blinded by tears' to visit Nancy and she would return to Sir Oswald, who did little to conceal his displeasure at her absence. The stress of the situation began to take its toll on her health.

When Sir Oswald died in 1980, Diana was diagnosed as suffering from a benign brain tumour and a successful operation cured her migraines. Diana felt suicidal when Sir Oswald died, and she often pondered a future without him; the thought of it, she felt, was too grim to bear.

JESSICA

Of course, I had been in love with Esmond for years, ever since I first heard of him.

– Jessica

Jessica spent her days cutting out press clippings of Esmond Romilly's adventures, asking mutual relatives about his exploits and reading his co-written autobiography, *Out Of Bounds*. When they finally met in 1936, Esmond claimed he had heard of Jessica through various friends and relatives, but in the back of his mind he did not take her attitude to communism very seriously; after all, many debutantes had flirted with politics only to forget their causes when the latest fad appeared.

On an early morning walk in the countryside, Jessica confessed to Esmond her wish to run away and how, in preparation, she had been saving up for years. Her Running

Away Account intrigued him. 'That's really fantastic!' Esmond enthused, and they quickly set about planning her escape.

When becoming involved with a potential suitor, it was Jessica's style to be upfront and direct. A typical conversation should follow:

Jessica: 'Esmond, are you going back to Spain?'
Esmond: 'Yes, perhaps, I think I'll be leaving in a week or so.'
Jessica: 'Would it be too much trouble to take me with you?'
Esmond: 'Not at all, but don't let's talk about it now.'

The circumstances of marriage, our constant wanderings about, the death of a baby, all had conspired to weld us into a self-sufficient unit.

– Jessica

Following Esmond's tragic death in 1941, Jessica threw herself into war work. In 1943, she met Bob Treuhaft, 'whose many attractions were his slanting twinkling black eyes, his marvellously funny jokes, his exotic Bronx idiom and pronunciation.' Their courtship was a stormy one and he was not what Jessica was used to. In the early days of their attraction, Bob and his roommate invited several of their female friends to town, and to Jessica's dismay, some of them showed up. Rather than being amused, Jessica felt intense pangs of jealously and, so disturbed by her feelings, she decided the best thing to do would be to leave for San Francisco.

San Francisco's vibrant nightlife held no mystique for Jessica and she found her surroundings Dickensian; her boarding house was grim and occupied by rowdy marines. Her only source of happiness came from Bob's chatty letters. Much to her delight, Bob cabled to say he was visiting San Francisco and, upon his arrival, Jessica bluntly asked him what his plans were. 'To marry you, and move out here to live,' was his equally blunt answer. They remained married until her death in 1996.

Apart from Deborah, Jessica was the only sister not to divorce. 'Could it be that I am, after all, the only one who is really settled down, as they say?' she wrote to Muv, with a sense of irony.

DEBORAH

Meeting him was the beginning and end of everything I had dreamed of.

– Deborah

Deborah met her future husband, Lord Andrew Cavendish, son of the tenth Duke of Devonshire, during the debutante season of 1938. They were seated next to one another at a dinner party and had struck up a friendly rapport. From that moment on they were inseparable.

The prospect of war was looming and men of Andrew's age knew that if it should be declared, they would be enlisted. But that did not stop Deborah and Andrew from gallivanting around London, and even in the uncertainty of war, they spent their free time dancing in nightclubs and dashing from one party to the next. 'We took no notice of the bombing – it never occurred to us that we might be hit,' Deborah recalled in her autobiography, *Wait For Me*.

Muv was concerned that Deborah was being hasty and advised her not to devote her entire attention to Andrew until he proved himself to be reliable. In the early days of their courtship, Andrew strayed from Deborah and showed interest in various beautiful girls in and around London. Deborah was heartbroken but felt elated when he came back to her. From then on, they decided they would be a couple and considered themselves to be unofficially engaged.

In 1940, on a visit to Andrew's parents' house, they became officially engaged. Her future mother-in-law, Mary Devonshire, had prompted Andrew to propose by warning him: 'You have either got to marry that girl or stop asking her here.'

In 1941, Deborah and Andrew were married at St Bartholomew the Great, London. The reception was held at Rutland Gate; the windows had been blown out during an air raid two nights before and sheets of wallpaper served as improvised curtains.

Since Andrew was not his father's heir, he never expected to inherit the bulk of the tenth duke's fortune and had pondered the idea of a career in publishing. However, Andrew became the heir apparent after his brother was killed in 1944. In 1950, Deborah's world was turned upside down when Andrew inherited the dukedom. Public life and service would follow, and they found themselves responsible for various stately homes, numerous staff and their families, and the onus of paying off the previous duke's death taxes, which came in at 80 per cent of the overall fortune, with interest accumulating at the rate of £1,000 per day.

As had his father and several members of his family, Andrew fought alcoholism and spoke frankly about his battle in his memoirs, *Accidents of Fortune*. With Deborah's support and his own willpower, Andrew managed to win the battle, and he remained sober for the last twenty years of his life.

Deborah and Andrew remained married until his death in 2004. She said of her late husband: 'Like everyone, he could be difficult, but like very few, he was never boring.'

—◈—

NANCY'S GUIDE TO

PLANNING A WEDDING

U Please note: A wedding is a sort of mental obstacle race.

U Choosing a venue is not a very difficult matter. Should one choose to marry in London, the ceremony should be held at the fashionable, Gothic church of St Margaret's, Westminster.

U Deciding on a dress is not so easy. Does one have it in satin, tulle or velvet? But an even greater problem is that of the skirt. One must avoid the Victorian or medieval appearance. Should one have a rich and thoughtful brother-in-law (Bryan Guinness), one should consult their opinion in a roundabout way. One might be on the receiving end of a generous gift.

U The perfect dress should be off-white, satin, with lovely pearl embroideries and a long train which forms part of the dress itself. I freely admit that white, the appropriate colour of a wedding dress, is very draining on Patrician skin.

U In the way of a trousseau, choose a dozen pairs of pink satin undies, which are more chic than crêpe de Chine, a dozen pairs of pyjamas and a few slips to wear under cotton dresses. If one chooses a small amount, one might be able to have lace on everything. Blissikins!

U Nanny might try to persuade one to add woollen nighties to the trousseau. One must decline.

U It is vulgar to have more than ten bridesmaids. Do try to balance this out with a small number of well-behaved children.

U Try to copy bridesmaid dresses from *Vogue*. Original dresses will cost a fortune and it is such a waste to pour a lot of money into the supporting cast. I would advise hundreds of yards of pearl-coloured tulle. The bridesmaids should aim to look like a flight of angels but must not detract from the star performer – the bride.

∪ Bridesmaids must be chosen for their good looks, the ushers for their well-known demonstration to the bride, and the best man for the air of calm superiority with which he meets all eventualities.

∪ A gift of a crystal necklace is perfect for the bridesmaids.

∪ The most tiresome obstacle is sending out the invitations. Who to ask? Shall we invite X? No, because that looks like we are fishing for a present and they are terribly sensitive about such things. But, on the other hand, if we don't invite X they will be offended. The dilemma!

∪ The guest list must be written in a little red carnet. To the list, add the names of those who have sent engagement presents.

∪ Finally the day has come for the bride to be squeezed into her wedding dress, primped and preened and poured down the aisle, only to have her make-up kissed off at the reception.

∪ When the bride leaves, everyone might stand around in a moment of demented calmness. At a loss of what to say, it is safe to make a neutral comment such as, 'Heavens, weren't they quick with the photographs!'

———

DEARLY DEPARTED

The sands are running out and of course we shall soon be dead.

– Deborah

At Asthall Manor, the children's nursery window overlooked the old churchyard with its wool merchant graves and beautiful tombs decorated with fleece and carved in stone. Deborah remembered: 'We were fascinated by funerals, which we were not meant to watch but of course we did.' Death was a fascinating topic for the girls, and they often wrote letters describing how they would give the other a nice send off when the time came.

In the 1950s, Nancy questioned her good friend, Evelyn Waugh, on the perils of heaven and hell and the resurrection of the soul. Evelyn, a staunch Catholic, tried his best to explain the technicalities of this great unknown procedure. After considering his point of view, Nancy summarised it in her own words: the resurrection of the soul was the equivalent to finding one's motor after a party.

MUV'S FUNERAL

I don't want a gangster's funeral, only a tomb.

– Nancy

Recalling Muv's death in 1963, Nancy remembered the 'marvelous' evening in accurate detail. The carpenter paid a visit to Inch Kenneth and measured up Muv's body for a coffin. The girls, who were in the other room, could hear the hammering of the nails as he secured the lid. It added an atmospheric touch, they thought.

The boat arrived to transport Muv's body to Mull, an eight o'clock sailing time, to be exact. The bagpipes wailed as the boat carrying Muv's body set sail for the mainland. The local men met the boat and accompanied the coffin on its voyage, all speaking in their native Gaelic tongue. A fleet of smaller boats followed. Nancy thought the maritime procession was 'too perfect in every way'.

Muv's death, not prolonged by her sympathetic Scottish doctor, seemed to Nancy as 'All *real*, not like when one dies at the London clinic'.

JESSICA'S DREAM FUNERAL

- The coffin of choice should be 'The Mitford' (see p.158) as it is both economical and stylish.
- It should be pulled by six black horses wearing elaborate plumes.
- A kind undertaker will carry out a good embalming job that takes six years off the corpse's appearance.
- The busy streets should be cordoned off and patrolled by police.
- Dignitaries won't be able to keep their composure and will resort to sobbing over the flower-covered brier.
- Proclamations should then be issued and 'that sort of thing'.

Despite her teasing, Jessica got a smashing deal on her cremation, no embalming and no frills. The total bill was $475. Her coffin was, in fact, pulled by horses, followed by a band and her ashes were scattered in the Pacific Ocean.

It's very curious dying and it would have many a droll amusing and charming side were it not for the pain.

– Nancy

THE MITFORD GUIDE TO THROWING A FUNERAL

Services are just for the survivors, when one's dead what difference can it make?

– Diana

✠ The main objective is to save money.

✠ Try to keep a level head when choosing the additional extras. If not, prepare to be exploited.

✠ Keep it simple and cast grandeur to one side.

✠ Choose a cheap coffin. If one feels quite pitiful about the cheap box, do recall the comforting words of Nanny Blor: 'No one's going to be looking at *you*.'

✠ Keep the service short; recall Farve's strict rule of allocating ten minutes per sermon.

✠ Old family favourites should form a suitable hymn repertoire: *Holy, Holy, Holy* and *All Things Bright and Beautiful*.

✠ The stalwarts will then haul the coffin over their shoulder and slowly walk to the graveyard where the loved ones are buried side by side.

✠ Sombre floods of tears will fall as the coffin is lowered into the ground.

✠ When the coast is clear, dry one's eyes and break into shrieks of laughter.

Sometimes I think the Church of England is the fount of all evil.

– Diana

Jessica & The American

Way of Death

I got pleasure from mocking these enterprises and the individuals who profile from them.
— Jessica on the attraction of muckraking

In Britain, death and dying were taboo subjects among the lower and middle classes. The upper classes, who were always matter of fact about everything, accepted death as a natural process. An excellent example of this acceptance is best displayed through Nancy's essay on U and Non-U language. Death was referred to, by the lower classes, as 'passed over' or any euphemism to avoid using the term 'died'. In the upper classes there was no skirting around the issue; it was simply referred to as 'dead'. Even in progressive America, death was a taboo subject among just about everyone.

Jessica sprung her subjects of death and dying on to an unsuspecting public in 1963. Her sudden interest in the funeral industry was provoked after a friend's husband died. Bob handled the funeral arrangements, at the request of the friend, and he found himself running into all kinds of strange expenses. Eventually, Bob founded a burial society in order to cut costs, but the undertakers fought back Jessica began to investigate and her findings developed into Jessica's book, *The American Way of Death*.

Jessica and Bob toured America, gathering information on funeral parlours across the country. She sent off for free samples from magazines, such as *Mortuary Management*, and received strange and wonderful things in the post: burial footwear, shape-enhancing underwear for the decomposing corpse and mouth shapers for when rigor mortis had set in. This seemed like a lark, but what Jessica was about to do as a result of her findings was vitally important. She exposed the money-making schemes which the undertakers were springing on the emotionally bereaved families of the dead.

When Jessica's 10-year-old son, Nicholas, died after being run over by a bus, she realised how the person sitting in front of the funeral coordinator felt. They weren't thinking straight and the funeral coordinator, a natural-born salesman, perceived how that person could be manipulated into purchasing non-essential extras. It was, as she discovered, a very wealthy industry whose foundations were built on emotional exploitation.

The entire funeral industry suffered because of Jessica's book. It became an instant bestseller; everybody in America was either reading it or talking about it, but most importantly, people began to readdress their views on the cost of dying. In an attempt to save the crumbling funeral industry, undertakers manipulated society with a psychological piece of advertising: 'How society treats its dead is a measure of their civilization.' This marketing slogan did little to restore people's views on the funeral industry when, in 1963, President Kennedy's coffin was a simple casket selected by his brother, Robert Kennedy, who had read and was influenced by *The American Way of Death*. To hit back at Jessica, the funeral industry invented a cheap coffin, aptly named 'The Mitford'. Following the book's publication, the popularity of cremation increased and people began to consider cost-effective ways of burial.

At a conference for the American funeral industry, Jessica was invited to speak before a panel of leading undertakers. A man approached Jessica and as he leaned down to kiss her hand, he announced: 'I only paid my dues to come here. It was $14,283 to be here this weekend, just to meet you, Jessica Mitford.' Jessica, amused by the man's enthusiasm, responded with, 'Oh you could have just given me the money and I would have come to you.'

The American Way of Death forced the American government to impose certain sanctions on the undertakers. In 1975, the Federal Trade Commission ruled that mortuaries must give consumers detailed price lists to avoid the trap of hidden charges.

Not only were corporations fighting back, Hollywood was jumping on the bandwagon. In 1948, years before *The American Way of Death*, Evelyn Waugh, an old friend and foe of the Mitfords, published his satirical novel *The Loved One*, which he dedicated to Nancy. The story, years ahead of Jessica's interest in American funerals, was based around the funeral industry in Los Angeles, the British expatriate community and the Hollywood film industry. *The Loved One* was adapted into a feature film in 1965, carrying the tagline: 'The motion picture with something to offend everyone!'

Following *The American Way of Death*, Jessica became an in-demand reporter, with popular magazines such as *Life* and *Harper's Bazaar* sending her on assignments ranging from interviews with movie stars (she got to spend the day with Elizabeth Taylor and Richard Burton) to going undercover at an Elizabeth Arden health spa. Jessica followed the success of *The American Way of Death* with further muckraking books, *Kind and Usual Punishment: The Prison Business* and *The American Way of Birth*.

—◦◦◦—

THE MITFORD GUIDE

TO WRITING LETTERS

✎ Personalised writing paper is perfectly lovely, but if one is caught in a recession, scrap paper or anything writeable is acceptable. Remember, it is the words that count, not the paper.

- Handwritten letters are a must; typing seems too formal and aloof. However, if one is cross with one's recipient, by all means type the letter.
- Always begin the letter with something wondair, i.e. 'Darling Crackinjay'. Do not write in a predictable manner: 'Dearest ... how are you?' That is so dull. For your convenience, here is a list of acceptable methods for addressing your recipient:

  - Dearest Anglo-Saxon.
  - Darling Bonehead.
  - Dear Madrigal.
  - Darling Stoney-heart.
  - Dearest Honkite.
  - Dear Cheerless.
  - Dear Hen's Egg.
  - Dear Fascist.
  - Dear Duchess.
  - Dear Squalor.

- The letter should flow like a conversation; this will allow you, the writer, to get away with being self-centred.
- Occasionally enquire after the other person, but only very briefly, and move on.
- Don't be ashamed to scribble out mistakes. This gives the letter a personal touch.
- Always end the letter with an open question or very vaguely. This will ensure a reply.
- If you are sick, make a conscious effort to bake the letter in the oven as this will kill any lingering germs. If you dislike the person you are writing to, by all means feel free to send the germs as well as your love.

☙ If you long to start a correspondence with all of one's sisters, do follow in the footsteps of Pamela and make an accusation towards one's sister and then abruptly announce that you will be off the radar for several weeks or months.

☙ An argument via snail mail can be most stimulating and will keep one entertained for weeks on end.

☙ A fax machine, as used by Diana, Jessica and Deborah, is perfectly acceptable if one is in a hurry or has urgent news.

☙ Nancy deemed airmail stamps as too common and believed it was very middle class to be in a hurry. Her letters took the longest to arrive but were so worth the wait.

☙ If a letter is incriminating or double-faced, always advise the recipient to 'tear up after reading'.

☙ If you are self-conscious about spelling mistakes, take advice from Pamela and keep a pocket dictionary handy. If all fails, spell the word it as it sounds: keeping the accuracy of the syllables will overcome most spelling mistakes. Pamela once spelled 'psychiatrists' as 'sechiatrises', and quickly added, 'I am at the Hairdressers so have no dictionary with me!'

☙ Use a dramatic phrase to close the letter. A list of acceptable closing endearments is as follows:

- I die for you.
- Very best Love.
- Much Love.
- All Love.
- In Tearing Haste.
- Cheery Cheer.

☙ Always store your letters in a safe place because, as predicted by Nancy, their value will increase over time.

☙ You will always be at the mercy of the postal service. Strikes are often as bad as a death in the family.

✒ Remember the long-suffering postman in your will. Jessica left her postman £5,000.

LITTLE KNOWN FACTS

Diana used green ink to write her letters. Why? Because Diana's little sons jumped into her bed every morning and the green ink was easy to wash out of the bedclothes.

Every Sunday, Diana and Deborah would speak to each other on the telephone. When she moved to France in the 1950s, Diana would telephone Nancy, but letters were always a priority.

It was Deborah's dream to be the elderly postmistress of a small village, and Diana's deciding factor in moving into her Paris flat was its prime location, conveniently located above a post office.

―∾―

PHRASES: MITFORD STYLE

As children, the Mitfords 'affected' way of speaking concerned their governess so much that she confided her worries to Muv. She told Muv that, should the children ever attend a day school, they would be bullied because of their unique turn of phrase and tone of voice. This concern did not alarm Muv, nor did she gently encourage the children to adopt a different voice. Such phrases have become as legendary as the girls themselves:

A howling orange in a black wig: Newborn babies.
A multi: A multi-millionaire.
Ballroom Communist: A term originated by Nancy to describe Jessica.

Blissipots: Blissful things.

Bloody: 'To behave perfectly bloody' is to be disagreeable.

Blor: The Mitford nanny's nickname.

Boud: Unity's nickname.

Cake: Deborah's nickname for the Queen Mother.

Chinless Wonders: Public schoolboys.

Debo: Deborah's nickname.

Decca: Jessica's nickname.

Do admit: Originated by Deborah to provoke a reaction.

Double-faced: Two-faced.

Extraorder: Extraordinary.

Fascinator: A fascinating person, thing or place.

Fat Friend: John F. Kennedy.

Fem: Lady Redesdale, often used as, 'The poor old Fem'.

Floods: To be upset/cry.

French Lady Writer: Nancy's nickname.

Frenemy: The girls invented this term to describe a friend whom they weren't fond of but continued to socialise with regardless.

Friend: Deborah's nickname for Prince Charles.

Henderson: A nickname shared between Jessica and Deborah.

Honks: Diana's nickname.

Honnish: A private language between Jessica and Deborah. Also a term used to describe a good deed/action: 'A Honnish thing to do.'

I note yr graph: 'I acknowledge your letter and I long to see you.'

In pig/pigging: Pregnant.

Kit: Diana's pet name for Sir Oswald Mosley.

Loved Ones: Favourite friends and family.

Mingy: Rather unpleasant.

Nevair: Never, such as, 'Well, I nevair!'

Nine: Nancy's nickname for Deborah, to describe her mental age.

Non-U: Not upper class.

Pigs: Babies.

Pygmy-peep-a-toes: Princess Margaret.

Sewer: Lord Redesdale's favourite insult for the girls' male admirers.

Shriek: To laugh, or as used in their letters, 'How I shrieked!'

Skeke: Mitford slang term for 'scarcely'.

Sir Ogre: Nancy's name for Sir Oswald Mosley.

Smacked one's ovary and sent to Madame Bovary: Pregnant.

Steake: Pamela's nickname for Jessica.

Susan: A nickname shared between Nancy and Jessica.

The Foals: Diana and Sir Oswald's youngest sons.

The Leader: Unity's nickname for Sir Oswald Mosley.

The Wid: Mrs Violet Hammersley, a friend of the family.

Trolls: Promiscuous men.

Tuddemy: A nickname for Tom Mitford, a combination of his first name and adultery, something which he indulged in.

U: Upper class.

Viz: Visualise.

Wife: A female best friend.

Woman: Pamela's nickname.

Wondair: Wonderful.

X: Used in sentences to describe one's conflicting feelings, i.e. 'Diana was very X about it'.

NICKNAMES

My mother's choice of nicknames for her children seemed, in some cases, to have been inspired with a certain amount of second sight.

— Jessica

The Mitford family was not in the habit of referring to anyone by their birth name. Since the day they were born and old enough to talk, the girls bestowed nicknames on each other, the more outlandish the better, and quite often the nickname originated from their first name or their appearance.

Nancy was named Ruby for the first few days of her life. Muv could not settle on the name and decided that Nancy's dramatic colouring of black hair and emerald green eyes reminded her so much of a pirate's moll that she appropriately gave her eldest daughter a name inspired by the Nancies of the sea-faring ballads – a reminder of Muv's nautical childhood spent on board her father's boats.

Pamela, an invented name from Sir Phillip Sidney's sixteenth-century poem *Arcadia*, which meant 'all sweetness', was an entirely suitable name for somebody who possessed no malice.

Diana was 'beautiful from birth', and she grew up to be a great beauty in the classical sense; her name, after the Greek goddess Diana of the hunt, healing and the moon, suited her so well. William Acton interpreted this image in his early 1930s painting of Diana dressed as the mythological huntress.

Unity's name was inspired by the timing of her birth, just days after the outbreak of the First Word War, and her parents' wish for unity between Germany and England – a premonition indeed. Her middle name, Valkyrie, was inspired by the Scandinavian war maidens from Wagner's opera *Die Walküre*. Wagner was also a great friend of the girls' grandfather.

Jessica's name in Hebrew meant 'foresight'. It seemed an appropriate name for somebody so passionate about changing the wrongs of society. 'You may not be able to change the world, but at least you can embarrass the guilty,' she said.

In Hebrew, the name Deborah translated to 'bee'. A queen bee, leader and prophetess – a fitting name for the eleventh Duchess of Devonshire, who would share the responsibility of reforming the Devonshire family seat, Chatsworth, a in doing so played a part in securing a family dynasty for generations to come.

However, of course, their given names did not last long and nicknames were quickly conjured up and each sister was labelled.

NANCY

Naunce: A diminutive of Nancy.
Koko: Nicknamed after the exotic character in Gilbert & Sullivan's opera, *The Mikado*.
French Lady Writer: This nickname came into practice after Nancy moved to Paris and adopted all things French.
Madame: Self-descriptive.

PAMELA

Woman: Because she displayed all of the skills associated with the stereotypical views of womanhood. This nickname was also shortened to Woo and Wooms.

DIANA

Honks: Diana's childhood nickname.
Cord: Pamela thought up the nickname of Cord, as in corduroy, for no apparent reason at all.
Bodley: Because of her large skull.
Nard: Unity's endearment for Diana.

UNITY

Boud: Jessica's nickname for Unity.
Bobo: Pamela used this nickname for Unity, despite Boud being the most popular.

JESSICA

Decca: Derived from Jessica.
Henderson: Deborah's nickname for Jessica, taken from their secret Honnish language.
Susan: Nancy and Jessica would often refer to each other as 'Susan' in their letters.
Steake: Pamela's invention.

DEBORAH

Debo: A diminutive of Deborah.
Nine: Nancy thought Deborah had the mentality of a 9-year-old and would often address her as such.
Hen: As with Jessica's nickname, this had a Honnish origin, derived from their invented childhood language.

THE LITERARY SCENE

Reflecting on her success as a novelist, Nancy confessed in an interview that she had written *Highland Fling* because she wanted to go on holiday to France but Farve refused to give her the money. This was a complete fabrication. Nar desperately needed the money. Her close friends were experiencing great success after dabbling in the literary scene: Evelyn Waugh's *Vile Bodies* was a bestseller and Bryan Guinness was writing his debut novel, *Singing out of Tune*. Nancy was friends with Hamish Hamilton, the famous London publisher, and this provided her with immediate access to the publishing world.

Her earliest books are nothing more than martini-and-cocktail-style stories, slightly plotless and with flimsy characters based, as always, on her nearest and dearest.

I've done five goodish novels, and three bad ones.

– Nancy

Nancy was a good storyteller: the dialogue was written in her light, chatty style and the text was brimming with witty jokes and private references aimed at those who were certain to understand the significance. But it has been said by her family and friends that had it not been for the need to earn money, Nancy's earliest novels would never have been written.

However, one affliction plagued Nancy: she could not spell very well, her grammar was often quite bad and she had no notion of the rules of punctuation. Evelyn Waugh tried to advise her, but his lessons were in vain: Nancy never grasped how to punctuate and commas in particular were her downfall. 'I do so try with grammar, but you see with me it's by ear. I can't understand the rules. My brain is a very uncertain instrument and I must only hope for a better one next time,' she complained.

I don't mind if scholars don't like them. I am writing to sell to large quantities and to amuse a lot of people.

– Nancy

Nancy had another peculiarity when it came to writing her manuscripts: she wrote them in longhand in a children's exercise jotter, which, upon its completion, she posted off to her publisher. Her publisher hired somebody not only to type the manuscripts, but to edit the text using the correct grammar and punctuation. Nancy referred to this person as her 'punctuator'.

> *I would like to become a good writer, and it should be possible because I have the exact temperament required, as well as some talent.*
>
> – Nancy

The success of *The Pursuit of Love* in 1945, followed by *Love in a Cold Climate*, was more than anybody had predicted. Nancy never quite matched their success in terms of sales or strong plots because, at the time, the characterisations of her loved ones were fresh and funny, the jokes were still original and the natural chatty style struck a chord with the post-war public. 'It was an exact portrait of my family and the character of my father and mother, absolutely exact,' Nancy confessed to an interviewer. When quizzed about her writing style, Nancy truthfully answered, 'I can't imagine Jane Austen writing about prisons in Siberia, she wouldn't have done it. Novelists always write about the people they know.'

The fictional novels that followed, although entertaining, were a challenge for her to write, and the forced plots and rigidness of the narrative are an example of her creative struggle. Diana said of her sister's later fictional novels: 'Nancy was good at writing about people she knew about, but when she got away from her own habitat, as it were, she wasn't so good. She had no idea about Teddy Boys or pop.'

From the mid-1950s, Nancy began to explore the nonfiction genre. Her historical biographies, *Madame de Pompadou*

Voltaire in Love, *The Sun King* and *Federick the Great* earned her respect as a serious writer. Some critics, unconvinced that she could write in an objective narrative, accused her of turning King Louis XIV of France into a characterisation of Farve and the entire Versailles court into the Mitford family. Deborah dismissed their claims: 'It was that lightness and quickness which made them so readable.'

Like snails, Nancy Mitford is a cultivated taste. Once a reader has acquired the taste, almost anything that comes from her pen proves edible. Sometimes she drips acid, at others, honey.
– *Montreal Gazette*, 1960

Jessica was as talented as Nancy, who made a career out of turning mockery into an art form, and when she published *Hons and Rebels* in 1960, Nancy and the other sisters were quick to notice a fictional undercurrent in her 'frank memoirs'. 'It is a dishonest book, full of lies and my sister's mind,' Nancy critiqued the book, and Diana added: 'We all know that *Hons and Rebels* is 90% lies and rubbish.' Nancy might have sided with her sisters in dismissing *Hons and Rebels*, but on the sly, she was praising Jessica and encouraging her literary career.

Fact or fiction, it did not matter: *Hons and Rebels* became a bestseller. It was perceived by the girls that certain remembrances of their childhood, although funny, came across as deeply offensive and caused a 'cold wind to the heart'. Evelyn Waugh noticed two voices in the narrative – 'Clever of you to see,' Nancy praised him. She suspected Bob had written half of the book, for, as Nancy accused, the expression 'cash in' was never 'off his lips'.

In 1950, Diana contemplated writing a book for her friends nd family called, 'Are you a Hon?', which was modelled on the

1930s book *All about Everyone*. The original book asked trivial questions such as 'Do you consider yourself good looking?' Diana modified the text with Honnish-related questions and several friends and family members filled it in. Sadly, the book was never published.

From 1953 to 1959, Diana edited *The European*, a far-right privately circulated magazine printed by Sir Oswald's publishing company, Euphorion Books. A collection of her essays and articles from *The European* were published in *The Pursuit of Laughter*.

Diana has often been called the true writer of the family; she was more intelligent than her sisters and her tastes spanned all genres of English and foreign literature. Her prose lacked the giddiness of Nancy's debutante narrative and Jessica's sarcastic tone, and she also became a popular author after the publication of her memoirs, *A Life of Contrasts*, in 1977.

Although she never became a much-loved public figure in the same light as Nancy and Jessica, people were fascinated by Diana's chequered past. In 1985, she followed up her memoirs with *Loved Ones*, a series of pen portraits based on her friends.

'The Mitford Voice', as Nancy labelled it, is prominent in all of the girls' writing. Whatever their talents may be, their unique way of telling a story and drawing on their rich and varied experiences has kept the public captivated since Nancy's first novel was published in 1931.

One must never write over the top.

– Jessica

—◆◆◆—

FRENEMIES

Every good feud begins with a frenemy – a friend who is an enemy. The term was invented by one of the girls when they were little to describe a 'rather dull' little girl who lived near them. 'My sister and the Frenemy played together constantly,' Jessica explained in *Poison Penmanship, the Gentle Art of Muckraking*. 'They were inseparable companions, all the time disliking each other heartily.'

The term frenemy, a seemingly modern word which slowly filtered its way into society through a variety of television shows, was actually first publicly used in Jessica's essay 'The Best of Frenemies', originally published in the *Daily Mail*, August 1977.

And, as Jessica advised in her essay, the term frenemy is 'An incredibly useful word that should be in every dictionary'.

NANCY & DIANA

You are divine to me. I don't know what I would do without you.

– Diana to Nancy

Nancy was the first sister to practise the fine art of backstabbing when she was on the receiving end of Diana's generosity following her divorce from Bryan. Without warning, she turned her back on Diana to pen *Wigs on the Green*, the farcical drawing room novel which mocked Sir Oswald's fascist ideology and Unity's love of Nazism.

Nancy, who was eager not to displease Diana but desperate to earn money, decided to press on with the novel regardless of the ill-feelings which were transpiring between the once-close sisters. Diana requested approval of the manuscript, and Nancy agreed that she could run her critical eye over the text.

Diana removed several catty jokes and unflattering descriptions of Sir Oswald, who was thinly disguised as the character of Captain Jack, leader of the Blackshirts. The protagonist, Eugenia Malmain, a large, eccentric heiress entranced by Captain Jack and his Blackshirts, was an exact portrait of Unity. In hindsight, this was perhaps Nancy's most satirical novel.

Unity was keen to stop *Wigs on the Green* from going to the printers. She was worried how her SS friends would respond to the book. 'All of the boys know you're my sister,' she pleaded with Nancy. Nancy promised Unity that the novel would be a flattering portrait. Although Unity had reservations, she hesitantly agreed and awaited its publication. Hardly flattering were the descriptions of Eugenia's 'batty' personality and overgrown physique dressed in 'ill-fitting' clothes. Unity, however cross she was, quickly forgave Nancy when a cheque appeared in the post, urging Unity to treat herself to some 'Nazi paraphernalia'.

Upon its release, Nancy tried to console Diana: 'The two or three thousand people who read my books, are, to begin with, just the kind of people the Leader admittedly doesn't want in his movement.' But Diana was livid and held a grudge for years. How dare Nancy mock her beloved Sir Oswald! Nancy was unfazed by Diana's estrangement; she disliked Sir Oswald and had little patience for fascism or Nazism. The sisterly devotion was wearing thin, and they drifted apart.

In the 1950s, when Diana moved to France, she and Nancy resumed their close relationship. Diana was the sister Nancy confided in and whose company she enjoyed the most. In return, Diana kept Nancy at arm's length; Sir Oswald disliked her and an air of mistrust always existed between the two.

UNITY & JESSICA

I don't see why we shouldn't personally be quite good friends, though political enemies.

– Unity to Jessica

Despite the political differences which had transpired between them, Unity and Jessica never feuded. Unity acknowledged they were 'political enemies' but she felt family ties ought to be different. Their love for one another was enough to bond them together without politics permanently severing their relationship. Jessica appreciated Unity's 'huge and glittering personality' and continued to reserve a special place in her heart for her beloved Boud.

EMPLOYMENT

Isn't work dreadful? Oh the happy old days when one could lie and look at the ceiling till luncheon time.

– Nancy

Apart from Nancy's freelance writing in the early 1930s, Jessica was the first girl to work for a living. During her months of living at Rotherhithe Street, Jessica landed her first ever job conducting market research for Esmond's advertising agency. Market research was considered to be a respectable job, slightly above selling or office work. The pay was higher and it was the kind of employment that might 'lead to something better'.

Jessica, with a team of market researchers, usually made up of ex-chorus girls and the wives of businessmen, would travel by train to manufacturing towns in the north of England or the Midlands. They received, in addition to their salaries, a small living allowance and their strategy was to find the cheapest accommodation available. The living conditions were squalid and they often slept two or three to a bed.

The objective was to compile information for the use of the advertising agency. The questions varied according to the product; some questions were fairly straightforward and others slightly more personal. Such intrusive questions – 'How often do you find it necessary to wash under the armpits?' – were usually met by a mortified housewife slamming the door in the market researcher's face.

After a day's work, Jessica returned to the 'feminine squalor' of their overcrowded room. She found her fellow market researchers, usually from lower-class backgrounds, to be alarmingly uncouth. She felt she had 'arrived at rock bottom of degradation', when night after night on such trips she endured their crude stories, always on the topic of sex and men, discussed 'without a trace of warmth or humour'. The market researchers opened Jessica's eyes to the realities of society and how other people, apart from her fellow political friends, conducted their personal lives. She was 'repelled yet fascinated' and hoped they were not the workers of the world 'destined to lead the revolution'.

Despite Jessica's disillusionment with the market researchers, she enjoyed earning money and doing a day's work, but was always glad when the assignment came to an end and she could return to the 'innocence and purity' of Esmond and the inhabitants of Rotherhithe Street.

In America, Jessica and Esmond drifted from job to job, mainly working in the retail sector. And in New York, Jessica worked in a smart dress shop on Madison Avenue and managed a Scottish tweed stall at the 1939 World's Fair. In 1941, they found themselves in Miami, Florida, where Jessica worked in a chemist selling 'sham' jewellery. Jessica landed the job on the false merit that she had sold jewellery at Selfridges department store in London.

> *Esmond and I have got jobs in a Miami bar, you must admit rather 'fascinating'.*
>
> – Jessica

After working in retail, Jessica tried her hand at bar work. The location was the Roma Bar in Palm Beach, Florida, where she worked alongside Esmond, serving as a cashier, general helper and was keen to learn the kitchen side of things. Esmond borrowed $1,000 to pay for a liquor licence and eventually he became a partner in the Roma Bar. They were content serving cocktails, chatting to the fascinating customers and mingling with rich tourists. For a brief period they lived in perfect bliss; young and popular, they made friends and adapted to their new surroundings.

However, eheir happiness was not to last. War was looming and Esmond would soon enlist in the Royal Canadian Air Force and be killed in action.

In 1941, months after Esmond's tragic death at the age of 23, Jessica enrolled in a secretarial course to learn typing and diction. Equipped with her new skills, she found employment as a secretary for the Royal Air Force Delegation in Washington DC. The following year, Jessica resigned and went to work as a clerk typist in the Office of Price Administration. Jessica gained a reputation for being a good worker and a quick learner, and she was promoted to the position of assistant investigator.

One afternoon, Jessica's future husband, Bob Treuhaft, spied her in the employees' canteen and curiously watched her as the lunch queue slowly descended. Jessica carefully moved along the counter, eating pieces of food before she made it to the cash register. When it was time to pay for her lunch, she had cleverly consumed most of its contents, thus greatly reducing her bill. Bob was impressed and thought Jessica was the most 'terrific female' the world had ever seen.

In the late 1940s, Jessica fulfilled her dream and joined a communist party in San Francisco. Though long past its glory days, it was the 'only game in town' in terms of civil rights. From then on, civil rights became Jessica's passion. Jessica worked for free as the party's secretary and devoted all of her spare time to the cause.

In 1973, Jessica was hired as a visiting sociology lecturer at San Jose State University. Her seminar included lectures on funerals and prisons, and as a bonus she included a seminar titled, 'The Techniques of Muckraking'. Her teaching gig was short-lived when she was fired for refusing to comply with a routine fingerprint test. Despite being fired, Jessica still showed up to teach her class and defiantly announced: 'They'll have to pick me up and toss me out to keep me from teaching.' The 250 students gave Jessica a standing ovation when she entered the classroom.

In her later years, Jessica would begin her working day at six o'clock in the morning, with a cup of coffee and shortly afterwards she would indulge in drinking 'delicious' vodka. Before an interview, Jessica would have a drink, usually vodka, as she felt it made her think clearer, calmed her nerves and clarified her mind.

In spring 1942, Nancy began working for Heywood Hill, a small bookshop in the heart of Mayfair, named after its owner. With Heywood Hill off at war, Nancy was responsible for running the shop. She arrived every morning to open the shop, dressed elegantly in a black velvet top and woollen skirt. She was a natural at selling books and had a knack for remembering obscure titles, publishers and prices, and was not shy of doing the hard labour of unpacking boxes, sorting out orders and lugging heavy parcels to the post office across town.

The bookshop, renowned for specialising in Victorian books and its appearance of a private house, with books stacked in no particular order on small shelves and spilling out on to the carpet, began to resemble a heaving literary salon. Nancy's friends periodically dropped in throughout the day to keep her company. Overhearing the gossip and shrieks of laughter that filled the shop, an irritated customer snapped, 'A little less "darling" and a little more attention to detail, please!'

However, not everything ran smoothly. Nancy forgot to lock the shop one Friday night and on Saturday morning she decided to sleep late. Customers noticed the shop was open and began to browse the shelves, all trying to buy books from one another. Luckily for his business, but unlucky for Nancy, Heywood Hill was passing through Mayfair and noticed the mad scene. 'He wasn't best pleased!' Nancy said.

The event was soon forgotten and Nancy began to dream up a business scheme to earn her enough money to go to Paris, where Gaston Palewski had returned the year before. She decided the best option would be to buy a share in Heywood Hill and open a Parisian branch of the shop. As part of her business scheme, Nancy would travel to Paris to source the books and sell them at a 30 per cent mark-up. Farve agreed to loan Nancy the £3,000 necessary for the venture, but as the war dragged on, the idea seemed less and less realistic. Nancy desperately missed Gaston, and she occupied herself by writing her latest novel, *The Pursuit of Love*.

The Pursuit of Love was completed in three months and had earned her £7,000 in the first seven months following its publication. Nancy, now a rich woman, could forget about her business scheme with Heywood Hill, resign from the shop and move to Paris. '*Vive la littérature*,' Gaston exclaimed as he arrived at Nancy's hotel room with a bottle of champagne to celebrate her success.

DECCA & THE DECTONES

It was sort of like a mad childhood dream to put this together. I'd always dreamt of being a torch singer but nobody asked me.

— Jessica

In 1995, after a bizarre series of events, Jessica briefly became a local pop star and 'ran off to cut a Rock and Roll record'. Jessica had originally sung The Beatles' hit 'Maxwell's Silver Hammer' with a kazoo band at a San Francisco nightclub to raise money for a local book festival. Jessica sang the chorus, 'Bang! Bang!' with such gusto that she was asked to do it again for Right to Rock, an anti-censorship campaign. The band became Decca & the Dectones and they held various gigs across San Francisco, with Jessica up on stage wearing a glamorous dress and belting out (or crooning) old songs. She sang the 1920s hit 'Mean to Me', wiping away false tears with a pair of men's boxer shorts.

Decca & the Dectones always pulled in a crowd but many of her contemporaries feared she was being exploited; however, this did not deter her and she continued on. 'Her wavering voice, once quite good, had deteriorated to a comic croak,' Leslie Brody, author of *Irrepressible, the Life and Times of Jessica Mitford*, wrote. 'Decca was having a blast and didn't care what anyone thought. She hit some notes, took a pass at others, but was always vivacious.' Jessica's friend, Maya Angelou, agreed: 'Decca doesn't have a lot of musical acumen. But on the other hand, she has the courage, the concentration, of somebody about to be executed in the next half hour.'

Bob, who was always supportive of Jessica's ventures, drove her to gigs and rounded up their friends, many in their seventies, to fill the audience to watch her perform, sing along and, most importantly, to lend their moral support. A short while later Decca & the Dectones recorded an album on an independent record label, appropriately named 'Don't Quit Your Day Job'. On the B side of 'Maxwell's Silver Hammer' was 'Help! Help!', a ballad Jessica used to sing with her sisters about a lifeboat heroine. The song was accompanied by crashing waves and seagull sound effects for the ultimate sea-faring experience.

Nevertheless, after a series of concerts, usually to raise money for local charities, Jessica found, at her advanced age, travelling to and from gigs was getting difficult and she retired from the stage.

5

HONS & COUNTER–HONS

THE HONS CUPBOARD

*My Dutch translator has written to say shall
he call the Hons Cupboard 'the cave of nobles?'*
— Nancy

The Hons Cupboard was a simple linen cupboard located at
the end of the landing in Asthall Manor. The hot water pipes
heated the small cupboard and, being the only warm room in
the house, the children flocked to there to keep warm. Jessica
and Deborah founded the Society of Hons, of which they
were the only two sworn-in members. As with many secret
clubs, the Society of Hons had an invented language known
as Honnish.

Honnish was a dialect consisting of north English and
American accents, combined together to produce a sound
which they dubbed 'Honnish'. In Honnish, the term 'hon'
meant 'hen', a nickname both Jessica and Deborah called one
another. Also, contrary to popular belief, Honnish had nothing
to do with the affixation of 'Hon.' before their first names.

Counter-Hons were the opposite of Hons and, therefore,
were excluded from the Hons cupboard. This rule usually
included the older siblings, but most definitely Diana, Nancy
and their brother, Tom. Later, the term Counter-Hon would

be applied to anyone who was not up to par with Deborah and Jessica's expectations.

Death to the horrible Counter-Hons!

– Society of Hons slogan

'HURE, HARE, HURE, COMMENCEMENT' – A HONNISH GAME

1. You will need two players.
2. The first player will pinch the arm of the second player.
3. Increase pressure and rhythm of each pinch while slowing chanting: 'Hure, Hare, Hure, Commencement' four times.
4. The player who can endure in silence until the fourth saying of the chorus is the winner.

BOUDLEDIDGE

Jessica's loyalties were divided between Unity and Deborah. With Deborah, she could indulge in childish games and her younger sister posed no threat to her political ideologies or her shocking behaviour. Deborah simply observed without criticism. However, with Unity she formed a loving relationship based on mutual respect for all things controversial. Unity and Jessica invented their own common language, known as Boudledidge, pronounced 'bowdledidge'. The secret language was unintelligible to everyone except Jessica, Unity and Deborah. Deborah could translate it, but she didn't dare speak it. Boudledidge served as a clever disguise for repeating scandalous stories and songs. An example was the risqué music hall song, 'Sex Appeal Sarah', which when translated into Boudledidge was called, 'Dzegs abbidle Dzeedldra'. Rather unintelligible, do admit.

———∾∾———

Tom Mitford

Tom, with his blonde hair, bright blue eyes and chiselled face, like 'a Saxon King', was said to have resembled a youthful version of Farve. He was born in 1909, a year before Diana, and their closeness in age and in looks made Diana think of him as her twin brother. Their close relationship was envied by Nancy, but all of the girls adored their only brother. He became a qualified lawyer and during his training he paid his youngest sisters to argue with him. Tom went to Eton and then to Oxford, and travelled extensively around Europe. He was a musical man and had studied classical music in Vienna, and the girls anticipated his fleeting visits to the family home, often bringing with him a fascinating friend.

He was always on speaking terms with all of his sisters but had been caught being double-faced on more than one occasion. When he was with Diana he was pro-fascist; when he was with Jessica he was pro-communist; and when he was with Nancy he was apolitical.

His visit to Germany coincided with the rise of the Nazi party, and the political party immediately captured his attention. He was impressed with their rise to power and how the party, once considered by many to be a band of thugs, had earned the trust of the German people and had delivered on their promise to rebuild the German economy. He related his tales to Diana, who was intrigued to learn more and to visit Germany.

Tom was charismatic and good looking, and had many affairs with debutantes and the wives of prominent men. His nickname, Tuddemy, given to him by his younger sisters, was a combination of his first name and favourite pastime, adultery. As a child, he once remarked to his grandfather, 'You know adultery …', and this became a common catchphrase among his sisters.

Tom adored Bryan Guinness and tried in vain to convince Diana to stay married to him. He was a frequent visitor to their house on Buckingham Street and moved in the same literary circles as the young married couple. He often acted as a go-between for Diana, and during her time in Holloway Prison he appealed to Churchill for her release.

After the outbreak of war in 1939, Tom joined the army but could not bear to kill Germans – some of his favourite people were German. At his request, he was posted to Burma where he did not mind killing the Japanese.

In 1945, Tom was shot by a machine gun and died on Good Friday as a consequence of the bullet wounds he had received in action on the previous Saturday. Pamela remembered her father crying openly at the news of Tom's death. The family never recovered from the loss, and Farve became an old man overnight. He used his bridge winnings to purchase memorial plaques, erected in Tom's memory in St Mary's church, Swinbrook, and Holy Trinity, the church on his estate in Northumberland. Both plaques are engraved with the Redesdale family motto: 'God careth for us.'

—✺—

Nanny Blor

Nanny Blor, whose real name was Laura Dicks, has been immortalised in Mitford folklore, and much like her infant charges, she was prone to eccentricities and possessed a unique turn of phrase.

Farve had fired the children's former nanny, known as Bad Nanny, for banging Nancy's head on the bed frame. And another nanny, upon seeing the newly born Diana, predicted, 'She can't live long'. Due to their lack of success with previous nannies, Muv was not overly enthusiastic when Blor showed up for an interview. Her credentials impressed Muv, but her slight frame caused concern. Muv worried that Blor would struggle to push the hefty toddlers' pram up the hill. Blor caught a glimpse of baby Diana and announced, 'Oh, what a lovely baby', and Muv hired her on the spot. She stayed for over forty years, and Diana reminisced in old age that she loved Blor more than her own parents.

Blor became a permanent fixture in the girls' lives and was the one they turned to for help and advice, never to their mother, who was said to be vacant to the point of neglect. She was such a strong influence in their upbringing that Nancy included a pen portrait of Blor in her 1962 book, *The Water Beetle*.

BLOR'S GUIDE TO LIFE

- To express disapproval, one should shrug their shoulders and haughtily sniff.
- When confronted by a show-off, never feed into their vanity and simply describe them as, 'Parading about.'
- If one should receive an unwelcomed question regarding one's age, wittily reply that you are, 'As old as my tongue and a little older than my teeth'.
- When someone craves sympathy from you, act aloof and announce, 'I don't pity you'.
- Upon seeing a young lady scantily dressed, as in Nancy's modern ball gowns, show one's disapproval by sombrely adding, 'You'll be cold'.

- 'Don't worry darling, nobody's going to look at *you*,' serves as a universal confidence boost for any occasion.
- 'I'm afraid nobody will like them when they are grown up if that's how they talk,' is an appropriate warning for the parents of children who swear.
- Blor was suspicious of Unity's trips to Germany and would say: 'I do wish you wouldn't keep going to Germany, darling.' *Sniff.* 'All those men!'
- Praises should be kept to a minimum. 'Very nice, darling' is quite ample.
- A strict warning of 'No, darling, I shouldn't do that if I were you' is enough to stop any delinquent in its tracks.

When Blor wasn't scolding the girls, she could be found immersed in the comfort of her deep religious faith, but unable to attend her own congregational church in Swinbrook, she never complained and practised in private. If the children had behaved especially well, they would have been treated to a bedtime hymn sung by Blor. All through Diana's adult years she found comfort in remembering Blor's favourite hymns. During her marriage to Bryan Guinness, and as a revered society hostess, she would gather her guests around the piano for an impromptu singalong from Blor's songbook.

BLOR'S MUSICAL REPERTOIRE

'Shall We Gather at the River?'
'The Ninety and Nine'
'Loving Shepherd of Thy Sheep'
'Now the Day is Over'

Mrs Violet Hammersley: 'The Wid'

*Child, they give a very curious sensation – I feel
as if I were walking backwards.*
— The Wid on country shoes

Mrs Violet Hammersley was a childhood friend of Muv's. She was born in Paris, into a wealthy family, and lived a lavish lifestyle during the opulent Edwardian era. She married young, to a rich banker twice her age named Arthur Hammersley and, when he died, she draped herself in widow's weeds which suited her sullen complexion. In accordance to her morbid appearance, the girls secretly nicknamed her 'The Wid'.

The Wid's pessimistic attitude served as a catalyst for brutal teasing from the girls, for she loathed happiness in all its forms and thrived on bad news. Her deep voice and hollow laugh, often provoked unwillingly, was an endless source of amusement to them. Upon hearing, or anticipating, bad news, the Wid rose to the occasion by wearing clothes in her favourite colour, black, and she was usually draped in gothic shawls, scarves and elaborate headwear which emphasised her dark, gloomy eyes. Ironically, Nancy recalled a trip where the Wid stayed with friends and they appropriately erected a sign inside their house which read: 'There is no gloom in this house.'

Once, the Wid expressed annoyance at Nancy's use of make-up by advising her: 'Painters don't admire make-up at all.' 'Oh, well Mrs. Ham you know it's all very well for you, but we can't all look like El Greco's mistress,' Nancy responded. To conclude the exchange, the Wid gave a hollow, unwilling laugh.

Nancy became a loyal penpal to the Wid and in her later years she patiently answered each letter, kindly taking the time to humour the Wid, who lived to old age. The Wid was fond of Nancy, and as she had done with so many people she admired, she bequeathed to her St Loup, her home outside Paris. Nancy was wise to this frivolous promise and suggested those in receipt of St Loup should form a union. Incidentally, her house on the Isle of Wight was known by the girls as 'The Isle of Wid'.

The Wid was a talented pianist. Her long drawing room had a grand piano at each end and she loved to play duets with musical friends. The girls admired the Wid's delicate hands, and on one slender, ivory finger she wore a diamond and emerald ring shaped like a fleur-de-lys. The girls coveted it and never hesitated, as children, to exclaim, 'Oh Mrs. Ham! Your ring! You are so lucky.' And they asked, 'Mrs. Ham, when you die will you leave me your ring? Please do.'

At a very early age, the girls discovered the consequences of the word 'lucky' when applied to the Wid. She considered herself to be the unluckiest person alive, and reacted accordingly to their reiterated cries. The Wid bestowed upon the girls the nickname 'The Horror Sisters'.

Unity was smitten by the Wid, and as a little girl she would sit perched on the end of the Wid's bony lap. 'Tell me, Child …' was the Wid's introductory phrase to anyone of any given age. Once the Wid announced her impending trip to Rome. 'Mrs. Ham is going to Rome!' the children exclaimed. Unity, quite out of the loop, asked, 'Where are you going to roam to?'

In the early days of the scandal caused by Diana's affair with Sir Oswald, the Wid travelled over to Rutland Gate about five times a day to visit each family member alone, to gather their personal opinions on the incident. Unity claimed the Wid was the only one who relished in the family scandal. The Wid also wrote to Nancy to complain about Diana being unchanged by misfortune, and to express her loathing of Diana's unwavering happiness.

Furious at not being included in Jessica's memoirs, *Hons and Rebels*, the Wid addressed her letters to Jessica, which she wrote in the third person, 'The writer of this letter …' She was also famously vague in her telegrams: in a bid to save money she often responded with one-word answers – 'yes' or 'no' – but never elaborated.

The Wid would not allow more than 2 inches of water to fill the bathtub; not only was she stingy with money but she could not stand other people using her hot water. Pre-occupied with other people's wealth, upon learning of Deborah's forthcoming wedding to Lord Andrew Cavendish, she implored: 'Tell me dear, will you be IMMENSELY rich?'

During the heavy rationing of wartime Britain, the Wid performed a Dance of the Seven Veils for the unsuspecting butcher who, in return, rewarded her with a small cutlet of meat.

As a joke to provoke Deborah, who adored the Wid, Diana and Unity formed the Anti Wid League and sent out recruitment letters to each sibling. In opposition to their tease, Deborah formed the Pro Wid League whose members consisted of herself, Nancy and Jessica.

Pro Wid League Rules

- Always pay the Wid's taxis.
- Always give the Wid any clothes she asks for.
- Always help the Wid with packing or with whatever chore is worrying her.
- Always buy the Wid's clothes off her at four times their price.
- Subscription is £500 a year which will go towards the Wid's upkeep.

LIFE WITH FARVE

These cigarettes are killing me by inches.

– Farve

If one is in doubt over how to channel Farve, one must remember one thing: to behave like Farve, one must fly into an uncontrollable rage at any given moment.

Farve wasn't one for sitting in a stuffy office or isolating himself from his vast offspring; instead he gathered up the children for a unique approach to the classic game of hide and seek. The children would trot off down the field and hide amongst the greenery. When the coast was clear, Farve would unleash his beloved bloodhound, a friendly domesticated pet, to hunt his children.

Deborah was his favourite child and together they would go off hunting, fishing and for long walks in the countryside. She shared his love of Swinbrook and the great outdoors, and this mutual appreciation bonded them together. That is not to say that he ignored his other children. Farve would go through phases of having short-lived favourites: one week it might be Nancy, the next it might be Jessica. One never knew who would take his fancy but pity always lay with the targeted sister whose turn it would be to experience Farve's wrath. The ill-feeling would often last for one week at a time, a constant cycle of children taking it in turns, all except Deborah, to whom his affection never wavered.

My father, who was a very clever person, in a way, quite uneducated himself; like a peasant. More like a very clever peasant. He could do anything with his hands; he had enormous

*hands like a peasant – he'd have been a marvelous
mechanician or plumber or gamekeeper.*
  – Nancy, interviewed for ABC Television, 1960

Farve possessed a quick wit and a superior sense of humour. At meal times, he and Nancy would sit opposite one another and fire jokes and insults across the table. The girls shrieked with laughter, until Farve bellowed, and Nancy fled the room in tears.

Unity's presence at the dinner table made Farve uneasy. She was almost 6ft tall, close to Farve's towering height, and would fix her cold gaze on him. 'Dammit!' he would yell. 'Stop staring at me!' As a response, Unity would slide under the table.

The girls adored the arts and once a year they were treated to a play in London, but a trip to the theatre was not without its grimaces. Farve was beside himself with rage in the car on the return journey from *Romeo and Juliet*. He was ranting and raving about 'that stupid boy' Romeo and Juliet's nurse, whom he described as a 'Dismal old bitch. She was probably an R.C.!'

Farve was mistrustful of artistic types, and he treated Nancy's creative friends with suspicion. In the mid-1920s, when it was acceptable for men to be outwardly vain in their appearance, a young male friend of Nancy's visited Swinbrook, a comb fell out of his pocket and Farve threw him out of the house.

Farve's masculinity did not seem strange to the girls until they began to socialise outside of the family home. Diana stayed at a friend's house and noticed her friend's father reading, openly, in the drawing room. Diana, intrigued by this seemingly odd trait, asked her friend why her father was reading – she had never heard of a man reading before.

Muv was alarmed that Farve had only read one book, *White Fang*, which he had found so good that he could not bring himself to read another. She decided to read *Tess of the d'Urbervilles* aloud, and as she reached the last sentence, Farve was in floods of tears. 'But darling,' Muv calmly reassured him, 'it's only a story.'

He exploded with rage, irritated that he had been emotionally disturbed by a piece of fiction. That ended Farve's literary pursuits. Farve disliked books so much he made it a rule that all books were to be confined to the library. There was to be no bedtime or recreational reading. Not within his view, anyway.

Farve possessed a will of iron, a trait he shared with Diana and Jessica. When Jessica eloped with Esmond, Farve disinherited her from his will and the two never spoke again. A brief reunion might have happened when Jessica made her first visit home in 1955; she told Muv that she would be willing to visit Farve providing he did not 'roar' at her family. Muv tactfully responded that since Jessica would see her father only with conditions, it would be best if she did not visit him at all.

Farve never warmed to his sons-in-law, and had his own unique description for each one: 'The *man* Mosley', 'The *boy* Romilly' and 'The *bore* Rodd'. Peter was an occasional feature, more so than Esmond who was in America and Sir Oswald who kept his distance. Farve asked Nancy, 'Why does he talk like that, with his mouth stitched up like a ferret?'

After more than a decade of estrangement, Tom's death in 1945 reunited Farve and Diana. Upon entering the drawing room, he greeted her warmly: 'At once, like the old Diana', James Lees-Milne wrote. Still under house arrest, Diana had motored down with Sir Oswald, followed by two policemen. She purposely failed to tell Farve that Sir Oswald was waiting outside. Farve, 'in his sweet, old-fashioned way', thought of the policemen outside and offered to send them out cups of hot sweet tea, the kind, he said, 'Policemen liked best'.

Diana managed to stall Farve from going outside. When it was time to leave, he offered to walk her to the car. Diana took him to one side and gently told him: 'Farve, the man Mosley is waiting in the motor for me.' Farve responded with a regretful smile.

In 1949, Nancy wrote to Evelyn Waugh, describing how Farve began to live for pleasure, especially for cocktail parties.

He even sold his cows because they interfered with the cocktail hour. His volatile temper had cooled and he became a much-mellowed, elderly man.

Money–Making Schemes

Farve owned a 'shack' on a 240-acre piece of land in Swastika, north Ontario, Canada, which he would travel to every few years to prospect for gold. He said of his venture:

> We do not rough it. The shack is completely equipped and we camp there while we are in Canada. I suppose from one point of view it might be called roughing. But I have been used to looking after myself for so long that I find nothing unusual about our Canadian trips.

Unfortunately for Farve, and for the ebb and flow of his dwindling finances, the land was not filled with gold.

Farve missed his chance to invest in something lucrative in the early 1900s, when a young inventor approached him with a machine that could make little blocks of ice in the home. 'Never heard such damned foolishness in my life!' Farve roared. 'Feller must be loony. Little squares of ice, indeed!' Farve had misjudged a golden opportunity to invest in ice cubes.

In the 1920s, an American man named Mr Reno approached Farve about a bizarre project, a sort of submarine tank which he produced the plans and blueprint for. When built, the 'Reno Tank' would be able to descend to the depths of the ocean and retrieve golden treasures from the seabed. 'Think of it – great chests of gold bullion,' Farve would say, gleefully rubbing his hands together.

Farve was enthusiastic about the project and raised additional funds from friends and relatives. Nancy, Pamela, Diana and Unity were allowed to invest £20 from their trust fund, which had been opened at the time of their birth and would grow to the sum of £100 by their twenty-first birthday. Jessica and Deborah, under the age of 7, were not permitted to take part in the venture.

All that glittered was not gold, and soon after Mr Reno absconded to America. 'Really *very* dishonest of him. I can't imagine what he must have been thinking of,' Muv said.

IMPATIENCE IS A VIRTUE

My father did not 'discriminate'. In fact, he was in general, unaware of distinctions between different kinds of foreigners.

– Jessica

In his own words, Farve disliked: Americans, frogs, foreigners and huns, other people's children and his children's friends and admirers. However, Farve liked a small selection of relatives and country neighbours. He despised the Duchess of Marlborough, not because she was an American, but because she had blown her nose on the dinner napkin and stuffed it in his garden hedge. The Duchess of Marlborough was banned indefinitely from visiting Swinbrook. Napkins were such an extravagance for the Mitfords that this gesture was the ultimate insult.

Farve had little time for lazy thinkers, simpletons or egotists. When Nancy started to bring gentlemen friends home from Oxford, Farve would bellow from the table: 'Have these people no homes of their own?' And often he would address the boys with his pet insult, 'sewer', derived from the Hindu word *sua* which translated to 'pig'.

However, if Farve was rather taken by one of Nancy's friends, he would greet them at the breakfast table with a fiendish grin and announce, 'Brains for breakfast? Pigs' thinkers!'

The dining table was a sacred object for Farve, and there was no room for error when dining with him. He could not abide anybody misusing the cutlery or spilling anything whatsoever. Staining the tablecloth was on par with insulting Farve. In his old age, and with his eyesight failing, Farve spotted a little boy across a vast, busy restaurant. 'Look at that degraded child,' he said to Diana, 'throwing its food over the good tablecloth.'

Farve was a meticulous timekeeper and did not tolerate lateness from anyone. He also liked to keep a tight schedule and set his stopwatch for ten minutes to time the Sunday sermons at church. He would signal to the uncomfortable minister two minutes before the allotted time was up. Farve, although a supporter of the Church of England, could not tolerate the trappings that went along with organised religion. In accordance to his preference for a timely sermon, Farve also warned the minister against selecting 'those damn complicated foreign tunes'. He liked simple, old-fashioned hymns. The sermon should also be without pomp and grandeur and he did not go in for 'smells and lace, incense, choir-robes and all that Popish nonsense'.

ECCENTRICITIES

It's a perfect nuisance – as soon as I arrive in London everybody wants to see me. I wish they'd leave me alone!

– Farve

On a Friday afternoon, after Farve received his pay from *The Lady*, he would go across town and buy the finest peach he could afford and present it to Muv as a gift. Muv consumed the peach after supper, usually offering him a bite or two, but twenty years later and long gone from *The Lady*, Farve discovered that she had, in fact, loathed peaches but kept it a secret as not to spoil the pleasure he received from giving her a gift. A gift which he thought was both economical and delicious.

One afternoon, on his return journey from *The Lady*, Farve spied a Shetland pony and decided it would make an ideal pet for his young children. He purchased the pony on the spot and ferried it back to their townhouse in a taxi. The pony was housed in a makeshift stable of straw on the landing until they moved to Batsford Park.

Farve, who was prone to superstitions, believed if you wrote a person's name on a piece of paper, and placed the paper in a drawer, that particular person would most likely die within the year. Did the drawer trick work? Farve never disclosed whether it did or not.

Farve took little interest in his daughters' education, viewing school as a waste of time for girls who, if they were sensible, would make a career out of marriage. Deborah remembered: 'With the slender profit from the chickens and eggs, my mother paid for a governess.' Some were hopeless, some very clever and one governess in particular taught the children nothing except how to play Racing Demon and they played it all day.

There was a reason behind Farve's dislike of school: he had an irrational fear that PE would give the girls thick calves, which he believed an unattractive feature which might compromise their marriage prospects. However, he did grant Unity permission to attend a day school, but she was soon expelled. Enraged by the school's action of expelling Unity, whose high spirits were not endearing to the curriculum, he threatened to throw the headmistress into the school pond. Needless to say, he relented.

Farve had a habit of carrying his worldly goods around in his pocket. Nancy remembered that he once retrieved a handkerchief from his pocket and a spanner fell out. She quipped, 'I suppose you've got a ball of string on you?' and he replied that he was moving with the times and produced some elastic bands.

Insults to Live By

A meaningless piece of meat: An unworthy person.
Degraded: Used in ways such as: 'Take your degraded elbows off the table.'
Go to hell judging your own time: Directed at an unfavourable individual.
Mournful: An insult directed at a pathetic person.
Sewer: Unfavourable young men.

Farve's Rules for the Breakfast Table

- Absolutely no spillage of anything whatsoever.
- Porridge must never drip from the ladle.
- Jam must never spill down the side of the jar.
- Arrive on time or risk not being fed.
- No one is exempt, not even children, from misusing the cutlery.
- The table cloth must remain clean at all times.

Muv's Medicines

If you're going to have it, you'll have it, and that's all there is to it.

– Muv on illness

'THE GOOD BODY'

Muv was suspicious of doctors and she detested medicine. She preferred to treat the 'Good Body' as naturally as possible, so when Jessica fell ill with stomach pains, Muv dismissed it as having consumed too much at breakfast. When Jessica could tolerate the pain no longer she took the initiative to telephone their family doctor, Dr Cheatle, to politely ask: 'Would you mind coming over to take out my appendix?'

After a medical examination, he diagnosed Jessica with appendicitis and declared that an emergency appendectomy would be necessary. The nursery furniture was draped in white sheets and Dr Cheatle anesthetised Jessica with a chloroform-soaked handkerchief. Farve was summoned to supervise the procedure. The operation was successful and Jessica's appendix was removed and placed in a jar for all to admire.

I suppose nowadays the surgeon would insist upon a clinic. Personally I prefer a brocade bed and beautiful unhygienic surroundings which (if one cares about such things) hasten recovery.

– Diana

Emergency operations were the only type of medical treatments allowed in the Mitford household. Muv looked upon them from a Biblical point of view: 'If thine eye offend thee, pluck it out' – in this case, if thine appendix hurts, rip it out! Muv quickly disposed of any medicines prescribed for the children: 'Horrid stuff! The Good Body will throw off the illness if left to itself.'

Muv harboured a complete mistrust towards anyone in the medical field, particularly doctors who, in her opinion, played God and pumped the Good Body full of germs. So, when

Jessica was ordered to undergo several weeks of bed rest, Muv hauled her up as soon as the anaesthetic wore off and encouraged her to do laps of the nursery.

Muv possessed an instinctive knowledge of the human body. Unlike today's society where holistic therapy is a mainstream practice, her views on the human body were thought eccentric during the early twentieth century. When Pamela developed polio as a small child, Muv denounced her medical beliefs and sought the help of six doctors in total and followed their individual theories on how to treat the disease. After being rebuffed by the disheartening news that nothing could be done for the ailing child, Muv turned to the modern ideas of a Swedish osteopath, Dr Kellgren, and permitted him to try out his ground-breaking theory of massage and exercise in a bid to cure Pamela. Surprisingly, Dr Kellgren's ideas worked, and Pamela, despite being slightly lame in her right leg, made a complete recovery from childhood polio.

When Deborah was stricken by measles, Muv scorned her joyful intake of antibiotics. To banish any lingering germs, Deborah baked her letters in the oven before posting them off. This practice supposedly killed any trace of the virus.

Ruptured organs, broken bones and contagious infections did not stifle Muv in the slightest. And when Jessica broke her arm, Muv tore off the doctor's bandages and made her do repeat exercises as to not let the arm grow stiff. Miraculously, her method worked and the bones righted themselves.

Fasting was also another medical theory which Muv overlooked, slipping the children pieces of bread and chocolate even though they were supposed to be surviving on a bland diet of water. Illness was not looked upon with sympathy either, whether it was chicken pox, smallpox, scarlet fever or the common cold. One must continue with everyday life in spite of it all.

Muv followed a kosher diet because she had a theory that Jewish people did not get cancer. She placed food into two categories: Wholesome Food, which she fed to her children, and Murdered Food, which was to be avoided at all costs.

One's body is very fragile, no doubt, but it's the only instrument we've got – better look after it.

– Nancy

Wholesome Food

    Wholemeal bread

    Organic eggs

    Chicken

Murdered Food

    Refined white sugar

    Flour with the wheat germ removed

    White bread

    Processed food

    Anything refrigerated

    Pork

    Sausages of any variety

    Rabbit or hare

    Every variety of shellfish

    Pasteurised milk

    Tinned food

And, keeping within Muv's views of the Good Body's ability to heal itself, Jessica advised a friend of a simple cure: a potato placed in one's bed or worn closely to the skin was an effective method of healing sore bones.

MUV'S MORAL CODE

Muv supported two causes – the Conservative Party and the Church of England – which meant the children, with animals in tow, had to attend church every Sunday. When questioned by Jessica on whether she believed in the afterlife or not, she replied, 'Well, one always hopes there'll be some sort of afterlife. I'd like to see Uncle Clem again one day, and Cicely, she was such a good friend of mine.' When reminded by Jessica that she did not believe in miracles, Muv justified her belief with a simple explanation: 'After all it *is* the Church of England, we have to support it, don't you see?'

Muv's Rules for the Nursery

- The window is to stay open day and night, 6 inches at the top.
- The children are not to eat between meals.
- The children are to be rinsed in clean water before getting out of their bath.
- The children are to have no medicine of any sort.

Muv's Words of Wisdom

Don't be vaccinated. I believe three out of seven deaths from smallpox in this old country are from vaccinations – terrifying.

– Deborah to Nancy

When Nancy suffered an ectopic pregnancy, Muv pondered: 'Ovaries – I thought one had seven hundred like Caviar.' After the operation, Nancy was concerned about the unsightly surgical scar, to which Muv flippantly replied: 'But darling who's ever going to see it?'

When asked by Nancy what childbirth felt like, Muv replied: 'Like an orange being stuffed up your nostril.'

Muv has been described by her six daughters as being abnormally detached. For example, one afternoon Unity flew into the drawing room, screaming: 'Muv, Muv, Decca is standing on the roof; she says she's going to commit suicide!' Muv responded without looking up from her letter-writing: 'Oh, poor duck, I hope she won't do anything so terrible.'

Muv treated vaccinations with contempt and argued against pumping germs into the Good Body: 'This silly germ theory is something quite new. The truth is doctors don't have any idea what really causes illnesses; they're always inventing some new theory.'

AFTERWORD

BEHIND THE SCENES

You see we're all saints now and we certainly weren't. It's quite easy to be a saint when one's old I note.

— Deborah

To the outside world and her fans, Nancy lived a lifestyle of utter bliss.

Deborah poignantly wrote, 'Isn't it strange to think how ninety-nine out of one hundred probably envied her.' Indeed, she possessed what many could only dream of: a spacious Parisian flat on the *Rue Monsieur*, custom-made clothes from the best French fashion houses, an elegant, unchanging figure and, as old age began to set in, she purchased a country house in Versailles, equipped with a rose garden and two pet tortoises. What more could one ask for?

Deborah followed up her statement with: 'Very few things went right, only the books I suppose and that is hollow compared to the real stuff.' Her fabled love affair with Gaston Palewski fizzled out after he married a rich divorcée in 1969, despite claiming it was against his religion to do so – the reason he could never marry Nancy. What made it worse was not so much his deception but the fact she had heard the news second hand.

Nancy tolerated many unpleasant things in her long affair with Gaston, including finding out he had a secret son, his indiscretions and the reality that perhaps he did not love her as deeply as she loved him. Only once did Nancy let her shop front slip, when she publicly berated him for his philandering ways. Was their affair anything more than a wartime romance which had settled into a comfortable friendship? We shall never know. Diana concluded: 'It just wasn't the sort of affair that leads to marriage.'

Nancy carried a torch for Gaston for the rest of her life. Although some might suggest that her death four years after Gaston's marriage was from a broken heart, it was actually from Hodgkin's disease, a rare form of cancer which had festered in her spine years before, eventually killing her in 1973.

My friends think I am terribly malicious.

– Nancy

On a brighter note, when not suffering from an unrequited love affair, Nancy travelled all over Europe, writing historical books and chatty articles for high-profile newspapers. She had earned enough money to write leisurely, and even though she had become a serious, in-demand writer, she was not above penning the occasional tease, often at the expense of her loved ones and sometimes at herself. She wrote her essay on U and Non-U language as a joke; it backfired and for the rest of her career she was labelled as a snob, and her name immediately became associated with that 'silly' essay. She admitted, 'Nobody knows less about etiquette and social etiquette than I do.'

I think Nancy was the most disloyal person I've met in my life. Of course, that is what made

*her such fun; she knew herself how disloyal she
was and freely admitted it.*

– Diana

Pamela found perfect happiness after her divorce from Derek Jackson in 1951. Life was often unpredictable with his volatile nature, and although she and Derek claimed to loathe children, Deborah believed that was a façade created by Pamela to fend off enquiring questions about why she did not have any children of her own. After her death, Jessica wrote to Deborah asking the same question, claiming that Pamela would have made a 'super mum' and, indeed, Deborah's daughter, Lady Emma, adored her. Pamela tried unsuccessfully to have a baby and in the end resorted to an operation to cure the problem, as had Nancy, but to no avail and she remained childless.

Pamela looked upon her dogs as her children and drove all over Europe with them, settling in Switzerland for long periods at a time, where she was the local star. Diana remembered that Pamela could not step outside her house without the locals worshipping her, and Pamela thrived on the warmth from the community, a love which was mutual.

In their old age, Pamela and Derek became friends, and Diana jokingly wondered if they would remarry. When Derek died, Pamela was astonished to discover he had left her a fortune in his will, and in true Pamela fashion, she was quite concerned that she could not write to thank him as it 'quite haunted her'. Pamela settled into a beautiful house in Gloucestershire with a much-admired garden, and she spent her days cooking, receiving visitors and visiting old friends in London.

Sadly, Pamela's life came to an abrupt end and probably sooner than expected. She had spent the day in London and was staying with an old friend when she fell down the stairs. After a short stay in hospital, recovering from an operation to mend her broken leg, Pamela regained consciousness and asked who had won the Grand National. A short while later, she went to sleep and never woke up. Until her death at the age of 87, Pamela had lived a contented life and was loved by all.

The awful thing is, as one grows older one minds less and less and lets everything pass.

– Diana

Although Diana lived a life of quiet exile in Orsay, France, with Sir Oswald, surrounded by her neighbours and devoted staff, history has not been kind to her. Unsurprisingly, her memoirs, *A Life of Contrasts*, was a bestseller which led to two more equally successful books: *Loved Ones*, a book of pen portraits of her nearest and dearest, and *The Duchess of Windsor,* a biography of Wallis Simpson. The press never forgave Diana for her past and she never apologised for her foolish views which she had adopted in her early twenties. Pride might have been the ruin of Diana, but her spirit was made of stronger stuff.

Diana lived until the age of 93, dying in her Paris flat, surrounded by her loved ones. Diana, who was so often described as unrepentant, claimed, 'I would choose the same life again, and in fact it's wonderful to be able to say that.'

However, just before her death in 2003, Diana confessed: 'It was a terrible thing to do, to arrest somebody with four young children simply because they'd had lunch with Hitler, but if I'd known it was supposed to be dangerous to do – nobody ever suggested it was – I suppose I would never have done it.' A friend asked Diana how she felt now the end of her life was in sight and she responded with, 'Remorse'.

Unity, the first sister to die in 1948, lived a sad life after her unsuccessful suicide attempt. The suicide was not a cry for help or a ploy to get attention; she had really meant to kill herself. On the day that she had planned to die, she posted a letter to her parents to say goodbye, left a note for Hitler and told her sisters of her actions.

Diana was the only one who believed her. Unity always threatened to end her life should Britain go to war with Germany, two nations she had loved so much – it had pained her to think of them being at war. On 3 September 1939, when Britain declared war on Germany, Diana had already feared the worst. Unity, in a deep anguish, walked to the English Garden in Munich, greeted a passer-by whom she knew, sat down on a park bench and put a pistol to her head. The shot from the pistol alerted the passer-by, who turned around to see Unity slumped in a pool of blood. But she lived, much to her dismay.

After a brief stay in a German hospital, Unity went to neutral Switzerland, where Muv and Deborah were waiting to bring her home. As a last nod to Unity's loyalty, Hitler paid for her hospital bill and the cost of sending her home to England. The two never met again, and the news of his death was kept from Unity, who lived in a haze of oblivion.

Muv and Deborah transported Unity home in a rattling ambulance carriage attached to the train. The jolting of the carriage hurt Unity's head, and for most of the journey she screamed in agony.

In England, she was met by hostile journalists who demanded to know why Unity had not been arrested for questioning. When asked for a quote for the newspapers, Unity peered from behind the blanket as she was being lifted into the waiting ambulance and announced: 'I am glad to be back in England, even if I am not on your side.' She was whisked straight to hospital, where an operation to remove the bullet was ultimately unsuccessful.

Unity lived out her final years on Inch Kenneth. Religion became her new obsession and she could be found in the dilapidated church on the grounds of the island, standing at the pulpit, giving sermons to an invisible congregation. In 1948, she died at the age of 34 after becoming ill from an infection caused by the lodged bullet in her skull.

Out of them all, perhaps Jessica suffered the most. She lost her first-born child, Julia Romilly, at the age of 5 months after a measles epidemic broke out in their neighbourhood, and her son, Nicholas Treuhaft, died at the age of 10 when he was hit by a bus. Jessica also endured the loss of her first husband, Esmond Romilly, when his plane went missing over the North Sea in 1941.

Always guarded about her personal feelings, she rarely spoke about the loss of her children and she never complained about the tragedies that struck her family. Opinionated and upfront in her writing, her second husband, Bob, often commented that Jessica bit the hand that fed her. 'But, why not?' Jessica interjected. 'The whole point of letters is to reveal the writer and her various opinions and let the chips fall where they may.'

Success did not change Jessica's views or her lifestyle. She became a best-selling author with the publication of her memoirs, *Hons and Rebels*, in 1960, followed by *The American Way of Death* in 1963. The latter book established Jessica's muckraking style of writing, using investigative journalism as a catalyst for her books. Success and fortune quickly followed. For the first time in her adult life, Jessica was well off and her writing gave her a voice to publicise her activist work.

Although they had a brief meeting over Nancy's deathbed in 1973, Diana and Jessica never mended their severed relationship. For a time after Nany's death they were cordial to one another, and Jessica made an effort, despite her hatred of fascism, to be civil to Diana. Diana, who was always ready to forgive and forget, was eager to keep up a relationship with Jessica and they briefly corresponded but Jessica abruptly stopped; she felt it was too odd to pick up where they had left off in the 1930s before politics had torn them apart. Diana, somehow, understood. They often asked after one another in their letters to Deborah, and Jessica wrote to Deborah to pass on her condolences when Sir Oswald died; she empathised with Diana for she knew how much he meant to her, but 'for obvious reasons' she could not pass on the message herself. Diana wrote to Jessica on her deathbed but the letter has not been published.

In her personal life, Jessica also suffered from alcoholism and was addicted to smoking, a habit which she failed to overcome. Determination and willpower helped her beat alcoholism, but the damage from smoking was already done and she died of lung cancer in 1996.

It is difficult to imagine the Mitford girls being extinct, even though their writing and legacy lives on. Deborah represents a forgotten age that we, who have not experienced it, often look upon with great affection. Not only has she been the chatelaine of one of England's greatest houses, Chatsworth, she was also the brain behind opening the very successful onsite farm shop. But, despite her successes in life, she has suffered from tragedy.

She suffered the loss of friends, including her brother, in the Second World War, and three of her babies died at birth; she supported her husband during his battle with alcoholism and outlived all of her sisters.

Deborah bemoaned the death of the stiff upper lip, the nation's dependence on therapy, their lack of common sense, living to excess and people living openly without morals, and the public's fascination for expressing every small detail of their private lives, which in her day was never openly talked about. She also acknowledged that nobody seemed to think independently for themselves and how modern society has done away with anything remotely eccentric – those facts which, she said, were the vital ingredients of individuality. She summarised her motto in life when she told an interviewer: 'Happiness was invented by the media.'

What is so nice and so unexpected about life is the way it improves as it goes along. I think young people have an awful feeling that life is slipping past them and they must do something – catch something – they don't quite know what, whereas they've only got to wait and it all comes.

– Nancy

Personal Recollections

Memories of Pamela Mitford

by Goldie Newport

My memories of Pamela Mitford go back a long way – fifty or sixty years. Of course I never knew her as Pamela Mitford. When I met her she was Mrs. Jackson and she came to live in Tullamaine Castle just outside the town of Fethard, Co. Tipperary, S. Ireland where I lived. We had the local newsagent's shop (which we still have) and she became a daily customer for her papers and magazines. We also had a second shop where we sold ice cream and confectionaries etc. She also visited that quite often and became friendly with my mother.

I remember her as a very quiet, country lady. She had pale skin, short blonde hair, which was straight and hung over one eye sometimes – Veronica Lake style! She seemed to live in a navy three-quarter length coat with brass buttons, a grey skirt and flat laced shoes – all very sensible but stylish, like herself really. In summer she wore a lighter flared skirt – linen or cotton, I suppose, of pale blue mostly to match her eyes, I suppose, and the most beautiful blouses I had ever seen and flat sandals. She never went in for fashion but always looked lovely and really simply 'classic.' I don't even remember seeing any jewellery of any kind not even a brooch or engagement ring.

Her husband Derek Jackson also lived at Tullamaine. He came and went but I never saw him. He was a physicist I've been since told but sixty years ago locals used to say he had a laboratory at Tullamaine, 'And lest the mercy of God he'll blow up the Castle and the whole of Fethard.'

Another thing which amused local people was a notice on the driveway inside their gates which said, 'DRIVE SLOWLY, PUPPIES, DOGS AND CHILDREN.' Irish people could never understand English people putting animals before children.

Mrs. Jackson had a little brown dog which she always brought to town with her. He was a little German Dachshund. We always called them dash-hounds – the long, low, sausage variety. He used to look so sad and anxious waiting for her in the car. Sometimes she took him out on a lead. She also always carried a square basket on her arm.

She used to bring eggs to town and sell them to one or two shops. My mother admired the basket one day and Mrs. Jackson said, 'It is rather lovely, isn't it? The German prisoners of war made it, the poor darlings.' My father, who was English, always referred to the Germans afterwards as, 'The Germans – the poor darlings as Mrs. Jackson calls them.'

Mrs. Jackson got on very well with my father. I think it was because he came from Gloucestershire, a place dear to her also. She used to say, 'Whenever I drive through Bibury, I think of dear Mr. Newport,' only she used to say, 'Mr. Noooport,' with her unusual elongated vowels and low accent.

Her gardener, Ted Young, used to sell us a beautiful box of mixed vegetables every week. I don't know how my mother got that privilege. It was the first time we were introduced to purple sprouting broccoli and it came from Mrs. Jackson's vast kitchen garden in Tullamaine. She always won prizes for her flowers and vegetables at the local shows. She was also a great member of our local I.C.A. (Irish Country Woman's Association) which she attended every month.

Mrs. Jackson once said to my mother when buying ice-cream in our shop, 'I can buy it cheaper in Cahir,' and my mother said, 'Then that's the place to buy it, Mrs. Jackson.'

A week or so later Goldie followed up this story with another fascinating account.

MUCH ADO ABOUT NOTHING!

BY GOLDIE NEWPORT

Mrs. Jackson had a friend, a young Swiss lady who used to visit Tullamaine every year. I think she came for the hunting season as she rode with the Tipp. Hunt and adored horses. She kept her horse in Larry Keating's stables here in Fethard. He was a trainer.

Her name was Miss Tommasi. She had very little English. She ordered the local Nationalist – a weekly paper, because she said it would improve her English!! After about three months she cancelled it because she said, 'I learn nothing. It is all ze dance, ze dance, ze dance.'

Another day she came into the shop in a very worried state and said, 'Please can you help? Where do I get a pig's face for Mrs. Jackson?' It seems Mrs. Jackson had sent her for a pig's head and she could not remember the name of the shop!

There is a woman, Marie. She is very interested in patchwork and all kinds of crafts. I asked her if she remembered Mrs. Jackson the other day and she said, 'No, I don't but there is a Miss Grant in Cashel who worked for her and she used to go to Kerry or somewhere every year to landscape gardens with her but that's a strange coincidence.

A few years ago I was at a craft fair in England for sewing etc. There was a woman there learning tapestry and she was having trouble with the threads. I offered to help her and show the little I knew. She was doing a beautiful tapestry of a stag in a woodland from a photo a friend had taken and sent to her. Anyway, she was most grateful for my help and asked if I'd like a job teaching tapestry. I thanked her but declined. I said I had more than enough to do at home. She asked me where I came from and I said Fethard, Tipperary, Ireland and she said, 'Oh, I had a sister living there in Tullamaine Castle. Her name was Mrs. Jackson. Did you know her?'

I said to Marie, 'You were speaking to her sister, The Duchess of Devonshire,' and Marie said, 'Is that who she was? I knew she was someone who lived in a big house somewhere near but sure that's all I knew. Is that who she was? Well, she was a lovely woman – very friendly.'

'Tis a small world.'

A Bid to Meet Decca

by Diana Birchall

My lifelong fascination with the Mitfords drove me, in 1995, to try to meet one. Singular as they were, I wanted to talk to and observe one of the sisters at first hand in order to have a better understanding of the family and the phenomenon. Also, they were getting older, and it was clear that if I was ever going to meet a Mitford, I had to accomplish it soon. As I live in Los Angeles, Jessica was the closest, but this was before e-mail and Google, and making contact was more difficult. I couldn't think how to track and meet her. Then a friend in San Francisco, intrigued by my determination, reported a sighting. Jessica was being auctioned off by the Berkeley Library – or at least a dinner with her was. My friend loyally bid $100. But a wealthy lady won the auction, for $700, the proceeds to go to the library, and this kind lady very generously arranged a dinner for eight, and invited me and my friend to be of the party. So I flew up to Berkeley and went to this elegant soirée at the lady's beautiful home high on the hills.

The amusing thing was that none of the other people invited (except my friend, and myself) really knew who Jessica Mitford was. They were just doing something nice for the library. Knowing that this was perhaps my only chance to ask a Mitford everything I wanted to know, I compiled a list of questions. What was Farve really like? Did Jessica get along with the others now? Were there really Nazi sympathies still in the family? How did she reconcile her lifelong love of communism with the fall of the Soviet Union? And could she demonstrate for me what the Mitford shriek sounded like? Superficial, perhaps, but the multiple biographies, *Letters Between Six Sisters*, and Decca's letters had not yet been published, and the Mitford reader did not know about the sisters' lives in such depth as we do now.

I found Decca sitting composedly alone and apart in the living room, a silver haired lady in her mid to late seventies, distinguishable from the other rather elderly ladies by her elegant finger-waved silver hair and the triangular, blue, baleful Mitford eyes. Those, I recognized instantly. The other ladies were gathered in little clutches, not liking to approach her, so I went up to her, plonked myself down on a footrest, and proceeded to ask my questions. She instantly lit up and opened out, answering every one of my questions in expansive detail. (She even gave me the Mitford shriek, which to my surprise sounded like a trilling little 1920s debutante giggle.) We talked for about an hour before being ushered in to the elegant dinner, and our lively chat continued during the meal, with the others looking on silently. Was I rude to hog her? But she seemed to like having somebody who knew about her and was interested in her stories. As for me, I was in heaven!

After the main course, the hostess, thinking she ought to say something, introduced Jessica formally to the group and then said, 'Now Jessica. We all know you came from England. Would you like to tell us what in your life brought you to this country?' The blue eyes blinked a bit in startlement, as of course she had by then been talking hard and animatedly about nothing less than her complete life story, for at least two hours. 'No,' she said, 'I don't really want to talk about myself, but I will tell you what I will do. I will sing you a song.' And she charged into a lively rendition of the Grace Darling song, with all the verses, followed by an amusing anecdote of how, when her family was on their island of Inch Kenneth, and they sang the song loudly with its chorus of 'Help! Help!' small boats would pull onto the island to see if there was any trouble. How she did know how to entertain – and to amuse!

The ladies, however, listened rather uncomprehendingly. After this rousing entertainment, another lady addressed Jessica earnestly, with, 'Jessica, I understand you have written a book called *The American Way of Death*.'

'I have,' said she.

'Well, I want to ask you this,' the lady said in a wavering voice, 'I am so concerned about this subject because – my husband, he is getting older, and it is just terrible – he is such a brilliant man! He has two college degrees! Tell me, Jessica, as an authority on the subject, do you believe there is an Afterlife?'

Jessica levelled her eyes at her questioner, not the eyes of a gentle elderly old pussycat at all, and said succinctly, 'No.'

My friend hastily interposed a general comment about how different religions believed different things, and Jessica raised an eyebrow and asked my friend what religion *she* was. 'Unitarian,' said my friend. 'Oh,' said Jessica, laughing, 'But that is really no religion at all, is it?' My friend laughed and conceded it.

Then to change the subject, Jessica announced, 'I think I will sing another chorus of the Grace Darling song now.' And she did.

I felt flattered that Jessica Mitford, my long time heroine, seemed to take such a shine to me, and actually asked for my phone number at the end of the evening. No doubt she did enjoy my interest. But I soon found out that she was also a canny organizer, and her method was to make use of people to achieve her various worthy aims. When she called and faxed me, she explained that her friend, Sally Belfrage, had died recently and prematurely of cancer, just after publishing a book about having been a Red Diaper Baby (a child of parents who were in the American Communist Party). Sally had not been able to do a book tour, so Jessica had organized a memorial book reading in San Francisco, and now she wanted one in L.A. She had an actress who was willing to have it at her house. Would I help organize, and as I was then the local Jane Austen Society president, invite everyone I knew? So I said I would, and Jessica came down to L.A. and invited me to lunch at her hotel, the Sofitel.

This was another very pleasant occasion with me asking her rather more serious questions. About her belief in communism after the fall of the Soviet Union, she said, 'Well, that is the problem, isn't it!' About fascism, she said heatedly that most of her family still did hate Jews really, and that was why she did not care to be among them much.

She did not come back down for the actual book launch, which was a rather strange occasion, since the spectacle of seventy-five Jane Austenites listening to excerpts of a Red Diaper Baby memoir was slightly surreal. But a lot of books were sold. I next saw Decca on a visit to L.A. when she invited me to a party at her lawyer's house, at which I met Maya Angelou and a delightful bevy of eighty-year-old communists and legendary screenwriters. My son came with me and it is one of his all-time cherished memories.

Soon after, the Duchess of Devonshire came to Los Angeles on a lecture tour, and I met her too. I cheerfully told her that I had won her sister at an auction, but she looked wary and alarmed – the look in the blue eyes, so similar to Decca's, was startlingly similar – and merely said, 'Oh really,' and backed away.

An Unexpected Mourner

by Debbie Catling

So, I decided to go stand in the churchyard at Swinbrook on the day of Pam's funeral and just wait and watch the mourners arrive. I was hoping to catch a glimpse of the sisters. I couldn't find anywhere to park, so I arrived in the corner of the churchyard just in time to see the last few people go into the church and the door close. I thought, as the flowers were all laid out in and around the porch, I would just nip over and take a look. As I approached, the pall bearers opened the door and ushered me in. It was never my intention to go in but I was too embarrassed to walk away, so in I went, clutching the order of service they had given me.

The church was packed and I hurriedly walked over to the one empty seat I could see on the end of a pew at the back of the small church. The funeral was lovely, quite short. To be honest, I can't remember much about the service. It was a while ago now, and I felt a bit flustered not expecting to be in there. Thankfully I was wearing a suitable dark coat and hat.

At the end of the service, the Vicar announced that tea was being served in the church hall while the immediate family were only to attend the burial in the churchyard. The woman next to me stood up and touched my arm and said, 'Excuse me, dear,' I turned and instantly realized that it was Diana and looked at the woman next to her and it was Debo. I think my shock must have shown. I had no idea I had stupidly sat on the end of the family pew (I knew it was at the back of the church, silly me). Diana thanked me for coming as I stepped aside to let her pass. Debo smiled and said, 'Do come to the hall for tea.' I was flustered and embarrassed all over again.

Diana was much shorter than I imagined, of course she was getting old now but her face was still stunningly beautiful. I think I said to you that I was sure the third person in the pew on the far end from me was Decca. She didn't leave the pew with the other two as she was talking to someone in the pew in front as Diana and Debo left. But in *Wait for Me*, Debo writes that Decca never saw Diana after Nancy's death, so I guess it could not have been her.

I suppose it was a 'you had to be there' moment. But it was a thrill, for this 'Mitty' to know that I had spent forty minutes in Swinbrook Church sitting next to Diana. I did not go back to the hall for tea. Obviously, I regret this now, but I felt pretty foolish having plonked myself down late in the family pew!

A Mitford Girl: Jessica 'Decca'

Mitford (1917–96) by Joseph Dumas

In the arc of a long-life, well-lived, The Honourable Jessica Lucy Freeman Mitford (1917–1996) pointed her moral compass towards true north. In her 79 years, that trajectory had catapulted her from Buckingham Palace – on the eve of the Second World War – where she had made her society debut; to an American Baptist church – on the eve of The American Civil Rights Revolution – where she had been held hostage, over-night, by a local terrorist network; to American graveyards, where she embraced the vicissitudes of the embalming arts and the commerce of the funeral trade; to American jails and prisons where she voluntarily permitted herself to be incarcerated; and, along the way, unwittingly, she discovered the scheduling habits of American obstetricians and uncovered mysteries surrounding the Northumberland heroine, Grace Darling.

All in a day's work for the 'Queen of the Muckrakers' – the only title she gloried in. *Time* magazine codified this daughter of the British aristocracy into the pantheon of such trail-blazing, investigative journalists, as Ida Tarbell, Nelly Bly, Lincoln Steffens, Sarah McLendon and Ethel Payne.

In consequence of Mitford's intrepid reporting, elements of American society changed: At the national level, the U.S. Government implemented The Funeral Rule which mandated guidelines of how the funeral trade conducted business with the public; and new attention was directed at the American penal system and also obstetricians and insurance companies. 'You may not be able to change the world, but at least you can embarrass the guilty,' she was fond of saying.

Were she alive with access to a pen, or fax-machine – not an iPad, not an iMac, nor even a PC – Jessica Mitford would be at her typewriter leveraging her various platforms (her books; her newspaper and magazine columns; the lecture circuit; private correspondence) to muckrake the issues of the day: the closing of the prison at Guantanamo Bay, Cuba; the political theatre of the American electoral process; Obamacare – the American president's health-care plan; and, oh, yes, the latest trends in American birthing and burial practices – the commercial aspects, of course. No doubt, she, too, would have joined the frisson against News International and its excesses in The Fourth Estate.

All that said, like her sisters, Jessica Mitford knew how to have a good time. Her life was not all Sturm Und Drang. Any cache of correspondence with family, friends, and professional associates crackles with the trademark language and cerebral wit peculiar to the Mitford sisters. She was known, for example, to fret over the proper passage of time to reply to fax-correspondence: 'Say, 15-minutes,' she once asked aloud.

No doubt, Jessica Mitford would have been interested in this project. Like her sisters, she was, by turn, both perplexed and flattered by the public's unwavering fascination with the family. When Mitford died in 1996, the English press speculated that Great Britain in the 20th Century could be witnessed through the prism of The Mitford Sisters. As a journalist, and in-concert with the aristocracy's un-flinching eye towards their histories, Mitford was at-ease in her family's story being revealed, as long as it was allied with the truth.

Between 1960 and her death, in 1996, from lung cancer, Mitford published 9 books. At the time of her death, she was engaged with her 10th book, an up-date of her 1963 classic, 'The American Way of Death' – or, as she would opine, 'Death Warmed Up.' In 1998, with the assistance of her family and friends, 'The American Way of Death, Revisited,' was released, posthumously. Mitford's books include:

'Hons and Rebels,' (aka, 'Daughters and Rebels') (1960)
'The American Way of Death,' (1963)
'The Trial of Dr. Spock, the Revd William Sloane Coffin, Jr., Michael Ferber, Michael Goodman and Marcus Raskin,' (1970)
'Kind and Usual Punishment: The Prison Business,' (1973)
'A Fine Old Conflict,' (1977)
'Poision Penmanship: The Gentle Art of Muckraking,' (1979)
'Faces of Phillip,' (1984)
'Grace Had an English Heart: The Story of Grace Darling, Heroine and Victorian Superstar,' (1988)
'The American Way of Birth,' (1992)
'The American Way of Death, Revisited,' (1998)

Since Mitford's death, two noteworthy books dedicated to her life have been published. They include her collected letters and an authorized biography:

'Decca: The Letters of Jessica Mitford,' edited by Peter Y. Sussman (2006)
'Irrepressible: The Life and Times of Jessica Mitford,' by Leslie Brody (2010)

What follows is an un-published interview (1993) I conducted with Mitford in London, England; and Oakland and Berkeley, California.*

(Background: Originally the interview had been commissioned by the American publication 'Modern Maturity' (the flagship magazine of the American Association of Retired Persons, aka AARP). At the time, the magazine was published monthly; however, it was the beginning of the period of austerity in U.S. magazines – which has continued, unabated – and the M.M. publication schedule shifted to bi-monthly. With a surplus of un-published interviews, the 4,000-word Question-and-Answer format was never published. Later, I was paid a kill-fee and the copyright reverted to me.)

Our conversation charts the broad-sweep of her peripatetic life: including her childhood in the English Cotswolds; her teen-age elopement with Esmond Romilly to Spain (during the Spanish Civil War) and the British Government's efforts to re-patriate her; her emigration to America – first, in Washington, D.C, then, later, the San Francisco Bay area, where she settled, eventually, in Oakland, CA, with her second husband, Robert Treuhaft, an American lawyer; a meeting

---

* recorded in London, England (Sept. & Oct. '93) and Oakland, California
  (Dec. '93)

with Prime Minister Winston Churchill in The White House; elements of the Treuhafts' activities in the American Communist Party, including their disillusionment; the launch of her literary career and its related investigations of the American social and commercial landscape.

As Mitford aged – despite having lived in America for a half-century, and by contrast to her politics – her tremolo voice and demeanor seemed to revert to the social class of her birth; and the legendary blue eyes, described by some as a cornflower blue – common to each of the Mitford sisters – remained undimmed.

JD: On page 478 of 'The Letters of Nancy Mitford,' Oscar Wilde's niece, Dolly, is mentioned. Charlotte Mosley said to ask you about her. What was she like?

JM: Bobo (Unity) and I met her through Nancy. We simply adored her and pretended to be madly in love with her – in fact, I think we were slightly. She had a large pale face just like Oscar Wilde's – looked exactly like him. Oh, incidentally, us being in love with Dolly made my mother furious. When singing to her music round the piano, there was a World War I song, 'Goodbye, Dolly, I must leave you …' ending 'Goodbye, Dolly Grey.' Bobo and I used to shout out 'Goodbye, Dolly Wilde!' causing Muv to slam down the piano.

(Background: It was winter of 1936, when we were all staying in Scotland. I'd written to Nancy saying how beastly it was there, and how the house was full of moribund flies – slow flies. That winter, terrible rainstorms were reported in Wales; also, a book called 'The Ladies of Langollen' about two famous 19th century lesbians had just been published. So, I got a telegram from Nancy: 'Flooded out of Langylolly. Traveling by slow fly. Dolly.' You can imagine how I cherished it!)

JD: Nancy Mitford promulgated a relentless tease on America. These shone through in her essays and letters. In her letter dated Aug. 4, 1959, she wrote, '… There's an American here called Wrightsman who talks exactly like Hector Dextor in my book. We get marks for the sentences we can make him say with the words "over a million dollars" but it's an easy game. He says Getty is hardly rich at all, not a penny more than 800 million dollars. Come & live in Yurrup Susan, come on, you'll never make 800 million dollars however long you stay there …' What did you make of her teases?

JM: Not surprising she loathed Americans – the ones she knew *and*, I might add, saw frequently were pretty ghastly, all except Art Buchwald whom she liked to no end and who made sport of her anti-Americanism. There were others who were mostly very, very rich tycoons whose unsuitably huge cars would take up the whole road in Rue Monsieur.

JD: On close reading, Nancy Mitford's letters to you take on political tones, certainly far more than in the general body. For example, in a letter dated Nov.15, '68 (p. 478), she wrote about a Czechoslovakian sojourn, then, the latter portion expresses chagrin at Sir Oswald Mosley's revisionism of his own history. Despite the light tone, her apparent seriousness shines through and seems a measure of respect. Please comment.

JM: The letter on p. 478: That letter caused a bit of a flap, as follows. Julian Jebb (BBC filmmaker) came out here to interview me as a part of his documentary, 'Nancy Mitford: A Portrait by Her Sisters.' Each sister was to read a bit out of one of her books and one of her letters. Julian had let drop the fact in a previous phone conversation that I needn't worry about the tastefulness of the program as my sisters Diana and Debo were in charge of vetting the final version! So I felt Diana might easily 'vet' out that letter. I told Julian that I should like him to read a statement that said, in essence, that if any of my part was to be omitted I would cancel the interview. All he had to do was to sign that this is what I told him – not that he agreed. This put the cat amongst the pigeons. His BBC boss rang up here to say that this was entirely against BBC policy. OK, said I, then I'll bow out of the interview. Boss rang back with a change of mind; so, it all went ahead. Have you seen the program? Worth having a look.

JD: Early on, Nancy Mitford seems to have flirted with fascism but finally laced her boots on the left. To what do you attribute this evolution?

JM: I don't think she ever flirted with fascism. This is due to an erroneous reading by Lady Selina Hastings (author, 'Nancy Mitford: A Memoir' (1986)). Nancy hated fascism – see, e.g., 'Wigs on the Green', hilarious take-off of Sir Oswald Mosley's movement. Also, when she went to Perpignan (France) to help relocate refugees from Franco.

JD: Jokingly, Nancy Mitford said she could trace the decline of the family fortunes by its addresses – i.e., from Batsford Park [Gloucestershire] to Asthall Manor [Oxfordshire] to Swinbrook House [Oxfordshire] to Old Mill Cottage [Buckinghamshire]. When you were a youngster, why did you want to run away?

JM: Well, for one thing, I was frightfully bored at home. We weren't getting any education and I didn't like country pursuits and we lived in the country. My sisters, for example – Debo, my youngest, adored all of that. She was a great rider, very athletic and she loved the country life and horses and the dogs. I was longing for a different kind of life, perhaps influenced by Nancy who was interested in intellectual things.

When I was about twelve, I was a frightful intellectual snob, let's face it. I think I'd read everything by Aldous Huxley and was always bragging to my cousins about this kind of thing, which was stupid of me, I admit now; but, on the other hand, it did open up a glimpse of life beyond Swinbrook, which, to me, was just a sort of dead end. I did want to go to college, to university, and, of course, there was no hope of going unless you'd have an education. So, as I told in one of my books, I bicycled to Burford which is about three miles from our house to see the headmaster of the grammar school – the free state school. I said I wanted to be a scientist. And they had a laboratory there and so I knew that they taught science. And I told him that I should love to come. And he said, 'We'll certainly consider you, but as you haven't been to school you would have to pass an exam.' And he gave me a reading list. I was frightfully thrilled. I thought, 'Oh, I can read that list in no time.' Then I went home and saw my mother. 'What a ridiculous idea!' she said when I told her I should like to go to university. She closed off; so, I threw the list away. And I thought, 'there'll be no escape.'

And Nancy, who was 13 years older, was still living at home. And despite the fact that she was a brilliant writer and a published author still hadn't got away. So, I thought the only answer to getting away is money. I started saving up a running away account. At Christmas, when we all had stockings, I would go through mine and sell my things to the other children. Everything I got I'd sell and so I accumulated quite a bit in the end.

JD: When did you first hear about Esmond Romilly?

JM: Early on because he ran away from Wellington [school]. He was the 15 year-old nephew of Winston Churchill and this was how he was always billed in the newspapers. We were almost a year apart in age. Needless to say, I thought that he was a thrilling example of somebody who'd run away and I should like to run with. Although he was a second cousin, I'd never actually set eyes on him, but he was kind of a hero to me. And then, much later on when he went to the Spanish War and wrote all those dispatches, which I've described in 'Daughters and Rebels' (1960). [The American title for *Hons and Rebels*.]

JD: Could your father really have affected an aid embargo against Basque refugees?

JM: It was the whole power of the British establishment. Those people stick together, you know, so he only had to say the word, although I don't think he knew Anthony Eden was the one who sent the destroyer to fetch me away and then I wouldn't go on it. [Initially] the British consul, Mr. Stevenson was away [from the British consulate] on business; so, the proconsul – the man who is a native of the country – was delightful. This fellow was from the Basque province of Spain; he was just a nice, sympathetic type, and, of course, he was on the side of the Reds in Spain, too. He showed us this telegram, saying, 'Jessica Mitford is a ward of the Court. Return her immediately.' We said you'll have to send a telegram back saying, 'I found her and she is not coming back.' Then when Mr. Stevenson got back he was a very different cup of tea. 'Look,' he said, 'if you don't return I'm just going to stop taking the refugees out.' We said, 'All right. We'll go. Goodbye.' And so we didn't go to England [but] to Bayonne [France].

JD: You and Esmond immigrated to America in 1939. What were you doing in 1941 when you learned his plane had gone missing?

JM: I was working in Washington and 'Dinky' [nickname for their daughter, Constancia Romilly] was a baby. I was living with the Durrs [Clifford and Virginia Durr] in Seminary Hill, Virginia. The whole idea was that we'd meet up in England as soon as I could get there with the baby. But that took some doing because there was all those U-boats, etc., and so, therefore, for a mother and child to travel required a huge amount of special authorization, or red tape. It so happened that on the very day I got my passage, I went to see some neighbors. Somebody came running back from the Durr House and said there's a telegram and Esmond was missing. So, we never went.

JD: Shortly afterwards, Mr. Churchill made his historic address before a joint session of Congress. He summoned you to the White House. What occurred?

JM: First, I had tea with Mrs. Roosevelt which was quite an experience.

JD: In what way?

JM: You're sitting there in a huge drawing room and so twenty people come in. They are, let's say, from the YWCA; then, she serves tea and they talk about their project. She takes it all in, and then, at a given signal, say 15 minutes, up they go, to be replaced by another group. It was very interesting to watch all that. Mrs. R. was terrifically interested in every sort of progressive project. I saw about three groups doing all that, because I was waiting to be told when I could go and see Cousin Winston.

Finally, I was taken upstairs [to the Queen's Bedroom] and there he was in bed, smoking a cigar, drinking brandy, wearing – I'll never forget – a wonderful peacock-colored dressing gown. I had Dinky with me. She was all dressed in white wool. One of the reasons I remember that was Churchill wrote to my mother and said the baby was dressed in white wool.

We started talking. The purpose of me coming was that I hadn't been able to find out what had happened to Esmond. I'd naturally thought he'd have escaped, he'd be in a boat somewhere, or taken prisoner, would be out soon, you know the feeling. I was keen to find out the precise fact. [Then] he started telling me all about the Mosleys who were then in prison, and how he'd arranged things nicely for my sister, Diana, which simply made me furious. We had a rather acrimonious moment. I said, 'I think they should be put against the wall and be shot.' They're traitors, and so, in other words, I wasn't being grateful for all that.

Then he said that his aide-de-camp could give me all the information about Esmond and the information was purely negative; in other words, there'd been a huge air search of the area. There was no hope at all. Then the aide-de-camp gave me an envelope which proved to have five hundred pounds, sterling. I wasn't pleased with that. [Later] there was a rumor going around in England – which was absolutely false – that I'd thrown the money at Churchill and said, 'Take it back' or something. I never did that. I thought money had value and I didn't want to use it for myself or Dinky, because it looked like blood money. So, I bought a horse for Ann Durr who was the 13-year-old daughter of Virginia, with part of it, and I gave the rest of it to the Committee to Abolish the Poll Tax.

JD: After your mother died in 1963, you have said that you found her diaries and saw notations about 'tea with Fuhrer.' What did they see in him?

JM: Oh God. It's almost unanswerable. Did you happen to catch a film called 'Remains of the Day'? Well, that kind of tells you a little bit. There was one great error in one of the reviews of the film. It said people like Lord Darlington [film character] always were opposed to the Versailles Treaty, which was holding Germany down, which is not true. On the contrary, they were the ones who imposed the Versailles Treaty. The Left and the Communists were the ones who thought it was a rotten idea to impose these huge reparations upon a defeated nation, because it could only lead to trouble. To put it very simply, that was it. So, we were all opposed to the Versailles Treaty while people like my parents were all for it until Hitler came along. And Hitler was a shining star. First, he outlawed the Communist Party. Second, he outlawed the trade unions which were always a thorn in the side of the Tories, and then, third, he was against the Jews. There was a huge amount of anti-Semitism in England. All you have to do is read a lot of English novels, beginning with Dickens, to get that feeling. It's sort of endemic in England; and so that was all right with them that he was crushing out the Jews. And the other thing, he was creating this marvelous youth movement which sound extremely attractive, where everybody had a job and was encouraged to do physical therapy and this attracted a lot of people.

JD: A lot of people have feared German unification. Now, there is the rise of neo-Nazi and Skinhead movements in Germany and other places. Is there something deviant about the German character?

JM: I wish I knew. The Germans are not my favorite people. All the things they are for, you know, sort of strict discipline; that sort of German mentality is not one that I like. But who knew where it was going to lead?

JD: With your family's access to Hitler, you have said you could have gunned him down. Had you actually hatched a plan?

JM: Not really; but I knew exactly what would happen; quite clearly, that would have been the end of me. And I'm sorry to tell at 15 or 16, I really wanted to live, which is rather weird I agree.

JD: Two of your sisters were known fascists. How did you come to be a member of the Communist Party?

JM: In the first place, the whole background of the Spanish Civil War. The international brigades, while not all Communist, were definitely led by the Communist Party. The fight against fascism, the impetus for defeating Hitler, came very largely from the Communist Party. [Plus a lot] was going on in England. The leaders of all the progressive movements were Communists. The unemployment movement was tremendous. The Depression was every bit as bad I guess as what happened in America. People in England were marching on London from faraway places like Wales where the coal mines were. They went into the Ritz, which in those days was only frequented by the very rich, and sat down and ordered tea. By law, they couldn't refuse. Things like that made all the newspapers. Then there was the Left Book Club run by Victor Gollancz, whose firm still publishes my books though Victor is long dead.

JD: What was the Left Book Club and its significance for you?

JM: The club sold Marxist and Communist Books. It was a fleeting thing before the war, let's say, from '33 to the start of World War II. The books cost five shillings each and the book club was to promote the books. Let's say a book had come out on Hitler. You would have a speaker and you'd discuss it.

JD: In 1943, you were working for the Office of Price Administration in Washington and, of course, this is where you met Robert Treuhaft. Both of you share Communist sympathies. How and when did you join the party?

JM: Well, first, Esmond and I didn't join the party in London as was widely believed. We were more at home in the left wing of the Labour Party. [Then] in Washington, there was no joining because it was so underground. If you asked a member, he'd immediately be on guard not to tell you anything. You can't imagine the intimidation. Then Bob and I got to California where things were much more open. That's when the head of the Federal Workers Union invited us to join. She's still a great friend.

JD: Your husband, Bob, once was listed by the House Un-American Activities Committee as being one of the most dangerously subversive lawyers in the country. Was he?

JM: Very! Subversive as could be! [Giggles]

JD: In what way?

JM: He was the General Counsel for the Civil Rights Congress in this area, when I was the Secretary and we worked together like mad all the time representing every aspect.

JD: In Oakland, California, you were brought before the House Committee on Un-American Activities. What was that like?

JM: I was never actually called. What happened was they would come into a town and stay maybe a week. They would subpoena a whole quantity of people but only call a fraction as witnesses. But they'd done the damage; every newspaper had every person's name, address and occupation. Everything was in the paper and tomorrow you were out of a job. Of all the things that were said and written about that period, almost everything concentrated on Hollywood and what happened to the writers. That, of course, is the natural thing; those are the glamorous, well-known people. But an awful lot of people were school teachers, librarians, rank-and-file union leaders; i.e., people with no political clout and no recognition. They were simply hounded out of their jobs. There were several suicides.

JD: You wrote to President Truman about what was going on, and he responded. Can you elaborate?

JM: I was Executive Secretary of the East Bay Civil Rights Congress. The CRC was a sort of militant defender of both free speech and black rights. These were things that put us at loggerheads with the powers that be. It was usual to see huge, flaring headlines: '100 Top Bay Reds Face Exposure in Probe.' That was 1953. Truman, himself, was threatened with subpoena, but he refused on the grounds he was an ex-President. It was a big story. I wrote him a long letter saying it's going to be just like Hitler's Germany. We in the CRC are being subpoenaed and now they're reaching into the Democratic party. If unchecked, they'll go on to destroy organized labor, the church, free universities and so on. Pretty soon there'll be no Democrats and we'll be ruled by the McCarthyites. I sent it off and thought no more about it. On the very eve of the hearing we got a handwritten letter from Truman that I've got framed in my study. He wrote: 'Your message in support of the Constitution of the United States and our free institutions is highly appreciated. Many thanks. Sincerely, Harry S.Truman.'

JD: How would you rate Truman as a President?

JM: People look back on Truman as being a wonderful old democratic bluff soul and all that. He wasn't at all. Actually, he was more responsible for McCarthyism than McCarthy was because he initiated the Loyalty Oath, which made the groundwork possible for McCarthy and that whole period. So calling it the McCarthy era is, to me, a misnomer. It should be called the Truman-McCarthy era.

JD: How did you come to know singer Paul Robeson during this period?

JM: He used to come out to the West Coast and stay with one of our best friends in Oakland. That's how we got to know him. This was when he was blacklisted and terrifically done down for being a Red.

JD: While visiting London in the 1950s, you contacted Lord Harewood, a cousin of Queen Elizabeth II, on behalf of Robeson. Why?

JM: His U.S. passport had been rescinded. My plan was to secure invitations for him to appear on the great concert stages of Europe in the hope that if enough were forthcoming from sufficiently august sources, his passport would be restored. He refused to accept this. He said he was not going abroad just to be a singer. He would only go if he could speak out against colonialism in Africa.

JD: You resigned from the Party in 1958. Why?

JM: Mainly because it came to a total dead end. The Khrushchev Report was extremely influential in driving lots of believers out of the party when they learned about the actual crimes of Stalin. I always felt I knew about the crimes of Stalin. As a girl, I'd read 'Darkness at Noon,' by Koestler, which described the trials of the subversives, the Trotskyites. My idea was that the Communist ideal should prevail in America and be an American indigenous thing; in other words, not having strings attached with the Soviet Union or any European Communist movement. The whole principle of Communism, Socialism is for the workers to have the means of production and everything flows from that. What was the Communist line on racism? Total equality of blacks and whites.

JD: Did it work?

JM: There were some white comrades who lived in neighborhoods where they were fearful their neighbors would do something drastic to them if they had black company. If they were having blacks to a meeting, they'd ask them to go around to the back.

JD: How did that go over?

JM: Obviously, that couldn't be tolerated in a movement devoted to equality. Then there were some extremely devoted, loyal communists, devoted to the idea of revolution. We used to call them the 1905ers; i.e. people who had come to this country from Russia, fleeing from Czarism, but they'd turn out to be absolutely hopeless on the matter of blacks.

JD: What do you think of the capitalist system?

JM: I think it's rotten. Why? Look around. You don't have to look far at the homeless [problem]. It's too long to go into, but obviously, it's a whole lifetime of noticing these things that leads one to these conclusions.

JD: Is there a more perfect political solution?

JM: Cuba? I've never really been there, but I wonder whether if it weren't for the blockade by the U.S., what might have been? Traditionally, socialism brings things like free health care, free education. Don't forget, by the way, that free education in the last century was considered incredibly radical. It wasn't a universally accepted idea for a long time. And don't forget the same is true of Social Security, which was initiated by the Left Wing, by the Communists and [was] bitterly fought by the Capitalists. So, there is a struggle going on in the world and one can only hope that it'll be resolved in favor of the people rather than the big-shots up-top who get all the money.

JD: *Esquire* magazine, in the early 1960s, sent you to the American South. What happened?

JM: I was writing an article about the white South and my whole purpose was to infiltrate the white South. It wasn't at all to have to do with blacks. This was 1961. And I was interested to see what made them tick, you know, what made them think the way they did. It was the time of the Freedom Riders. As I'd done all the border states, I then went to Montgomery, Alabama and I was staying with Virginia Durr, and we had driven up to the Durrs' country place in the woods [for the weekend].

And when I was there, the Freedom Riders came and their bus was burned in Anniston, Alabama. And so you can imagine, every time you turned on the radio you'd hear nothing else. Everybody was frightened and nervous. And on our Sunday return, there was a radio broadcast, say, in fifteen minute intervals, 'Tonight there's a meeting of Martin Luther King and the Freedom Riders at the Baptist Church and nobody knows what's going to happen.' This was a clear incitement [to riot]. We could tell what's going to happen.

That night we had dinner at Virginia's house and she'd invited some students to dinner. One of the first students to arrive was Peter, a white boy from Antioch College. He was doing his work-study. So, I said to Viriginia, 'Could we possibly borrow your car and whip down to the church for a second or two, just to sort of have a look there and see what's going on?'

She said, 'All right.'

So I said, 'Peter, come on, do let's go.'

'I don't want to get in any trouble,' Peter said.

'Trouble,' I said, 'don't be silly. It's a church. Couldn't be any trouble.'

Someone said to park several blocks away because you don't want anything to happen to the car. We arrived and as soon as we saw what was happening, I said, 'Let's park very close to the church. We might need to get out,' because there were these white mobs all in white mob clothes set for trouble. Peter and I were dressed up in proper things; he had on a suit and tie and me – white gloves and a hat. We just walked through the mob and into the church. I can't remember now if we said we were friends of the Durrs or what, but we were ushered in and put square in front. The church was maybe supposed to hold a thousand and it seemed there were two thousand – babies, young and old people.

On the dais were Martin Luther King and Ralph Abernathy. King got up and said the church is now surrounded by mobs who were out of control, and the marshals who were supposed to guard the place had been beaten back. In consequence, there wasn't very much protection. And there was the frightfully depressing smell of tear-gas. People near the windows were coughing and choking. Then the television people folded their tent and left. Chickened out. We were the only whites there, except for Calvin Trillin.

Martin Luther King was saying, 'Don't look back. Keep your eyes straight ahead.' Obviously, everybody was looking around like mad. He said, 'Keep quiet and don't panic.' He really was great. He actually kept you mesmerized with singing and uplifting and at the same time leveling with everybody that you might not ever get out alive, which was the feeling. And the church was quite wooden. So, if they had tried to torch it. Quite depressing.

Somehow, they got through to Robert Kennedy and soon the National Guard appeared.

King announced a getaway plan: All those who had come by car would be followed and escorted. The others would be driven. It was getting on 5:00 A.M. I wanted to call the Durrs whom I knew had been listening to the news all night. I finally got up to where King was, and, of course, he knew the Durrs quite well.

I said, 'We're staying with the Durrs. I don't want to go to their house and lead the mobs there. Could you tell me the name of a hotel in Montgomery where Peter and I could go until dawn and then get a taxi home?'

He said, 'The Jefferson Davis.' It was so funny, somehow.

Meanwhile, there'd been an announcement that one of the marshal's cars had been burned to a crisp – only it turned out it wasn't one of their cars but the one we'd borrowed from the Durrs. So, it was arranged by King and others that Peter and I were going to be taken by the National Guard to the Jefferson Davis Hotel.

The guards were like the Freedom Riders; i.e., about 15 years old. They had guns and I said to them, 'Put those away.' 'Yes ma'am!' they replied.

When we got there, they started to come in after us but I said, 'You can go now!'

'Yes ma'am!' they replied.

Later, the fire marshal came to the Durrs house about the burned-up car. He said to me, 'Are you a member of the NAACP? And do you go to that church regularly?'

I said, 'None of your business! Your business is to find out who burned up the car. Good-day!' I was quite annoyed. And it was all in the paper.

You'll be wondering what happened to Peter. He came round first thing the next morning to say, 'Goodbye.' He said, 'I'm going with the Freedom Riders to their next destination,' which was Jackson.

JD: You converted him.

JM: Yes. Complete. And so there he was in jail the next day.

JD: How do you think Dr. King should be remembered?

JM: With enormous pride. I can't imagine anybody who contributed more. If you read the history of the time, he was the moderate, and people like those in the Student Non-Violent Coordinating Committee were the advanced guards who were really fighting the battle. But they eventually ended up very much together. And to the degree that they didn't end up together was largely the fault of the thinking of the SNCC people, of being too narrow-minded.

JD: In 1963, you published 'The American Way of Death.' What led you to write about this topic?

JM: Actually, it was Bob's idea. He was a trade union lawyer who represented the longshoremen. He began to notice that whenever the bread-winner of the family died, the amount of the death benefits – hard fought for through union struggle and [intended] for the widow and kids would mysteriously be the price of the funeral. He got furious and started organizing the Bay Area Funeral Society, a non-profit educational group which also has a contract with an undertaker for a fraction of the price. I thought the whole thing was rather boring. We were robbed everyday by the landlord and at the supermarkets, so why bother about the undertakers. Then he started bringing home the trade magazines like 'Casket and Sunnyside,' 'Mortuary Management,' all those wonderful names. So I began to study them.

First, he got me to write an article but nobody would publish it. It ended up in a small, liberal democratic magazine in the Oakland area. He had it re-printed in lots of 1,000 to give out for propaganda for the funeral society.

All kinds of developments started from there. Here's one really one odd thing. Casper Weinberger, in those days, was a liberal republican in San Francisco. He had his own weekly television program called 'Profile-Bay Area.' He did one [segment] on the Funeral Society. There were four [guests]: me and a Unitarian minister on one side and two undertakers [on the other side] whose actual names were Mr. Sly and Mr. Grim. It caused a huge stir. [Subsequently,] *The Saturday Evening Post* did a long article called, 'Can You Afford To Die?' [As a consequence] they got hundreds of letters addressed to me because of having been on that program. Raoul Tunley was the author of the article in the S.E.P. We said you really ought to write a book about this. But he didn't want to. So I did!

JD: In the book you said embalming is not essential, even for public health.

JM: No, otherwise, why wouldn't they have it [as law] in other industrialized, developed countries like England or Germany? They don't.

JD: Then why is it always done?

JM: Tradition is what undertakers have decreed. They say you've got to be embalmed and be a beautiful memory picture!

JD: What about coffins? Are they necessary?

JM: No. There's no law and no health reason either. But no cemetery will take a body unless it's in one. They make their own rules.

JD: You wrote in your book that cremations became hostages of the funeral trade. How?

JM: The funeral industry began to see they were getting nowhere by refusing cremations, which they did at one point; I mean, they would do everything to talk the family out of it. But if you can't lick'em, join 'em. Now what they are doing is to push the sale of funeral urns like mad, which is really killing! There's a marvelous article in a recent 'Mortuary Management' issue in which the advice is to divide up the ashes amongst the children and each child gets a wonderful, hand-crafted, beautiful, expensive urn. And I think it went so far to say there was actually, practically a civil war among the siblings all vying for which could have the best urn. They'll do anything to get a buck.

JD: How were funerals handled in your family?

JM: My mother died on the Island of Inch Kenneth, off the Scottish mainland, which is pretty remote, so the carpenter came. He measures up the person for a coffin, makes a coffin, the person is put in the coffin. Everyone had to go by boat to the Island of Mull. There's a tradition there of other boats following. So all these people who lived on other islands in the Hebrides came. Apparently, it was a rather beautiful moment. Then she was kept in a chapel in Mull overnight. The next day, she was taken by motor hearse to the South of England, to Swinbrook, where she was buried.

JD: No embalming?

JM: Oh no.

JD: What rights do consumers have in negotiating with funeral directors?

JM: The Federal Trade Commission passed a rule that took away some of the funeral industry's pizzazz. For example, [funeral homes must] give you a price list; they can't give you an overall price based on the price of the coffin. They've got to break it down so you can refuse anything you don't want. If you don't want embalming, you can say no. If you don't want a slumber room or whatever, you can say no. Then they've got to reduce the price to whatever it is you want.

JD: What kind of funeral do most people want?

JM: Nobody knows what the public wants. If you ask the man on the street, the response is like, 'As far as I'm concerned, they can throw me in the Bay to feed the fish. I don't think we should spend money on funerals. It's more important to spend it on children's education.' But when they [die], they're in no position to talk back.

JD: Did coffin manufacturers really design one for you?

JM: They've threatened to, but I don't think they've done it. I did get plans and specifications from a Midwestern manufacturer for a Jessica Mitford casket. It was a cheap wooden affair or made of plastic!

JD: Have you made any funeral plans for yourself?

JM: What I should always tell people is I only want the best because the embalmers can shave 20 years off your looks. You can be a beautiful memory picture lying in a silk coffin and [have] six black horses with white plumes [to carry you away]. You know, there is the feeling that one should plow some of one's profits back into the industry. But then I'm afraid that when the time comes, my survivors are going to burn me up and throw me out! And so then I'm afraid all my dreams will come to nothing.

JD: What general advice would you give to people wanting to pre-plan their funerals?

JM: Don't pay any money down. Do not give the funeral director anything; more people have been robbed that way. Funeral directors simply put all the money in their banking account. They may disappear out of your life completely, long before you die. And why do it? If you want to make that sort of an arrangement, set up a trust with the funeral director as your trustee. Then he can get the money when you die. But you keep it. You have the use of it and you have the option of firing him anytime you like. This is one of the worst rackets in the whole funeral industry. So, the idea is to arrange for a cheap cremation, or the best way, the absolute fool-proof is to donate your body to a medical school. All organs should be useful to the living, like eyes, etc. You are always reading about people who need transplants of every kind of thing. All you need is to make clear what you want.

JD: You received a Guggenheim Fellowship to study America's prison system. In 1973, your study, 'Kind and Usual Punishment' was published. Do jails deter crime?

JM: No.

JD: Do jails rehabilitate?

JM: No. The only examples of rehabilitation are of people who have plowed themselves up of their own determination; a very good example being this fellow Dannie Martin. [He] and Peter Sussman, an editor at 'The San Francisco Chronicle,' have written this book called 'Committing Journalism,' which has just come out. For years, Peter Sussman had been publishing Dannie's articles from behind bars. Dannie Martin is an example of somebody who's totally rehabilitated as far as I can see. He's now got his own real profession. He's an excellent writer and he's a journalist.

JD: For your research, you entered a prison as an inmate. What was that like?

JM: Jolly unpleasant I can tell you. The worst of it is in the women's prisons. Women prisoners are treated as sort of horrid little girls who have done something naughty. They're not treated as bad as the men, but there's a great condescension in there.

JD: The paperback edition of 'The American Way of Birth' recently came out. So many things have happened on the health-care scene since it was first published that you had to add an afterword.

JM: We might call it an 'afterbirth.' In the first place, nobody had heard the expression 'managed competition' until [the paperback came out] so I had to explain all that. Also, there's been a lot happening on the 'midwife front' in California. Legislation [may] legalize them in the same way they are in Texas and New Mexico.

JD: How did 'The American Way of Birth' evolve?

JM: It really started with the case of Janice Kalman, a mid-wife in Chico, California. [She] was performing marvelous things for the families she served. Never a breath of criticism or that she had harmed anyone. [Next thing], she was being investigated with a view to criminal prosecution by the Medical Board of California, which is really a sort of disgraceful offspring of the California Medical Association.

JD: What was the charge?

JM: Practicing medicine without a license.

JD: Why do you believe she was so charged?

JM: Money. In other words, the mid-wife charges one-tenth of what the doctor-hospital combined is going to charge, given ordinary birth.

JD: Your book also rails at Cesarean births. Why?

JM: It's unbelievable to the rest of the world that in America one out of every four babies is a Cesarean. Cesareans were an incredibly important invention in the last years of the 19th century to save the lives of mothers and babies in danger. And before that, Cesareans had always been performed but always on dying mothers or dead mothers to preserve the baby, but there was never a case where both mother and child survived. Nobody is knocking Cesarean as an idea. There are rare cases where this is absolutely essential. But the cases are rare. I found out towards big holidays like Thanksgiving or Christmas there were some doctors whose Cesarean rates rise to 70 per cent because they want to get away; [this is] much to the doctor's convenience and financial prosperity to whip the babe out at his own timing.

JD: Why does America have such high infant mortality?

JM: It has to do with poverty and with absolute neglect of people. Neglect. There is no pre-natal care available to many people. We've found this out [in the Bay area] and you'll find [the problems] doubled in rural communities. America's infant mortality rate is among the highest in the developed countries. And among black people, seventeen births out of a thousand, the baby dies before a year; for whites, eight [out of a thousand births die].

JD: Do you foresee the Clinton Health Plan addressing this?

JM: In my view, the single payer proposition [would] address this properly. In other words, where we cut the insurance companies and have everything administered by the government, [whereby] the government makes an agreement with the doctors about how much you pay. This cuts out 25 per cent of the total cost, which, largely, are administrative costs and profits by the insurance companies.

JD: What do you think of the President's health-care reform?

JM: In my book [I recall a] joke going round that Wilbur Cohen, Secretary of HEW under LBJ, once asked God if the U.S. would ever have a national health insurance. 'Only if I live long enough!' God replied. We have to wait and see. [Clinton] talks about universal health insurance, but then when you study [the proposal] you don't find it. The main thing I see is its shortcomings.

JD: Hillary Rodham Clinton once clerked in your husband's law firm. How would you rate her performance taking on health-care reform?

JM: I think she's been marvelous. The thing is, she's in a trap. She can't support single-payer because politically [its supporters] feel it can't pass. But on the other hand, the more they can do to get public opinion up for it now, the better chance there will be to pass it somewhere down the road. There's always some ridiculous opposition based on the magic word 'socialism' or 'socialized medicine.' Doctors capitalize on the term. People will be against it because they think it's socialized medicine. Well, you have to remember the same argument was made against Social Security and certainly, against the trade unions; it's a bloody uphill battle, but until we have single payer – and by the way – there are apparently 93 Congressmen supporting single-payer.

JD: Do you think the legislative process will evolve single-payer?

JM: Only if there's a huge consumer demand, enormous popular insistence. That's the answer. Polls show that the American public are for single-payer, preponderantly, and, depending on the polls, somewhere between 60 and 70 per cent.

JD: Why, then, is it politically impossible?

JM: Because of the huge amount of campaign money poured in by what one member of the Hillary Rodham Clinton Task Force called 'The Evil Empire,' which is the whole medical community, the insurance industry and the pharmaceutical industry.

JD: Recently, Surgeon General Joycelyn Elders called for the legalization of drugs. Do you agree?

JM: That's my answer in view of the frightful things going on in America now; i.e., the drug addictions, the killings. If you legalize these things, make them totally legal; give them free to addicts, which takes out the criminality and the enormous amount of money involved. Legalization would be the thing. The typical heroin addict in the early part of the century was a white, affluent, middle-class woman whose doctor prescribed the drug. It was only in 1913 the first repressive laws against drugs came. [Not long ago] in England a registered drug addict could get his fix from the National Health Service. The London addict population was stabilized at 3,000. In New York, the same population is estimated to be 30–40,000.

JD: How do you see race relations in America today?

JM: They are pretty awful again. Most of the dreams of the Sixties haven't been realized and racism is absolutely flourishing as we can see everywhere; and I think the right wing is posing a great threat.

JD: To what do you attest the popularity of someone like Rush Limbaugh?

JM: There's always been a very deep fascist strain in America, always has been ever since I've lived here. That's all hand-in-hand with the Klan and all the most rotten aspects of American life.

JD: Do you detect differences in race relations in your native England and America?

JM: Not really. The English have always been racists. I would say that Britain is the cradle of racism. Don't forget that the wealth of Britain was built on Colonialism; and therefore, the whole theory of colored people being a different race and an inferior race went along with that; it's all economic at root. When there was a big influx of blacks into England right after the war from various parts of the empire, that was when overt racism really started in England because before, there was nobody to be racist about within the country. [As a child], we lived near Oxford. My vision of black people were these scholars; you'd see them walking around in their scholarly robes and whatever they wear in Oxford, a University town. I'm not sure where they were from – Africa, I imagine. But if you saw a black person in the street, say, in London, everybody would turn around and look because that was rare.

JD: Recently, you lectured in Mississippi. How did it feel after your earlier experiences?

JM: One of the people I met there was a white lawyer married to a black woman. We all went to lunch and there were a couple of black lawyers, too; and the idea that we could walk into a restaurant and just sit down and have lunch was so amazing. And you could practically see the outlines of 'White Only' on the lavatory doors. It had just been whitewashed over.

JD: Name someone who influenced you most and steered your activist career?

JM: I suppose it would be Esmond. Then, also somebody like Philip Toynbee. These are the people I identified with and socialized with when I was a girl.

JD: Who could you name as having known that you are most proud?

JM: Maya Angelou would come towards the top; and someone like Cedric Belfridge. He was editor of an American socialist journal, 'The National Guardian.' He had been deported from America for being a subversive. He did lovely, good things.

JD: Who would you say have been some of the other great muckrakers?

JM: One that I've only heard about now is Nellie Bly. I think she's in that collection that Harvey Swados did on the muckrakers. The early ones are Ida Tarbell and Lincoln Stephens. I didn't know much about the history of it all, but there's a fascinating book coming out soon about Nellie Bly.

MITFORD BIBLIOGRAPHY

I really never will read any more beastly books they are only an extra complication to one's pathetic life.

— Deborah

NANCY MITFORD

Highland Fling, 1931
Christmas Pudding, 1932
Wigs on the Green, 1935
Pigeon Pie, 1940
The Pursuit of Love, 1945
Love in a Cold Climate, 1949
The Blessing, 1951
Madame de Pompadour, 1954
Noblesse Oblige, 1956
Voltaire in Love, 1957
Don't tell Alfred, 1960
The Water Beetle, 1962
The Sun King, 1966
Frederick the Great, 1970
A Talent to Annoy: Essays, Journalism and Reviews, edited by
Charlotte Mosley, 1986

Love from Nancy: The Letters of Nancy Mitford, edited by
Charlotte Mosley, 1993
The Letters of Nancy Mitford and Evelyn Waugh, edited by
Charlotte Mosley, 1996
*The Bookshop at 10 Curzon Street: Letters between Nancy
Mitford and Heywood Hill*, edited by John Saurmarez Smith,
2004

DIANA MITFORD

(Published as Diana Mosley)
A Life of Contrasts, 1977
Loved Ones, 1985
The Duchess of Windsor, 1980
The Pursuit of Laughter, edited by Martin Rynja, 2008

JESSICA MITFORD

Hons and Rebels, 1960
The American Way of Death, 1963
The Trial of Dr Spock, 1970
Kind and Usual Punishment: The Prison Business, 1973
A Fine Old Conflict, 1979
The Making of a Muckraker, 1979
Poison Penmanship: The Gentle Art of Muckraking, 1979
*Grace Had an English Heart: The Story of Grace Darling,
Heroine and Victorian Superstar*, 1988
The American Way of Birth, 1992
The American Way of Death Revisited, 1998
Decca: The Letters of Jessica Mitford, edited by Peter Y.
Sussman, 2006

DEBORAH MITFORD

(Published as Deborah Devonshire)
Chatsworth: The House, 1980
The Estate: A View from Chatsworth, 1990
The Farmyard at Chatsworth, 1991
Treasures of Chatsworth: A Private View, 1991
The Garden at Chatsworth, 1999
Counting My Chickens and Other Home Thoughts, 2001
The Chatsworth Cookery Book, 2003
Round and About Chatsworth, 2005
Memories of Andrew Devonshire, 2007
In Tearing Haste: Letters Between Deborah Devonshire and Patrick Leigh Fermor, edited by Charlotte Mosley, 2008
Home to Roost … and Other Peckings, 2009
Wait for Me!, 2010
All in One Basket: Nest Eggs, 2011

FILM & THEATRE

Count Your Blessings, a feature film adapted from Nancy Mitford's novel *The Blessing*
BBC2 Playhouse, Unity
The Mitford Girls (a musical)
Jessica Mitford: The Honorary Rebel
Nancy Mitford: A Portrait by her Sisters
Love in a Cold Climate: A miniseries
Nancy Mitford: The Big Tease
The Mitford World
Diana Mosley: Adolf, Oswald and Me
Hitler's British Girl

Unrealised Projects

In 1932, Diana was almost cast in *The Winter's Tale*, when C.B. Cochran, the show's potential producer, had the idea of surprising the public with a new face. He offered the part to Diana and she was flattered and felt inclined to accept. Diana's friend, Dr Kommer, heard of the idea and immediately went to Cochran and talked him out of it. Diana's acting debut came of nothing and although 'rather cross' about it, she admitted, 'No doubt Kommer prevented me from making a fool of myself'.

Nancy was hired by Ealing Studios to work on the feature script of *Kind Hearts and Coronets*; however, none of her writing survived in the final cut of the film.

In 1947, David Lewis sought the screen rights for *The Pursuit of Love* to be produced by Enterprise. Vivien Leigh was considered for the role of Linda but pre-production stopped at the last minute.

In 1949, Nancy wrote a film based on a small boy who attempts to keep his parents apart. The script was refused and Nancy developed the idea into a novel, *The Blessing*. Ironically, the rights were bought by MGM and the film was retitled *Count Your Blessings* and was released in 1959, starring Deborah Kerr and Rossano Brazzi.

In 1954, MGM offered Nancy $6,000 to travel to Hollywood and work on the script, *Marie Anne*, adapted from Daphne du Maurier's novel. Nancy's intense dislike of America, although she had never visited, caused her to decline their generous offer.

Television writer Ian Curteis had planned a film based on all six Mitford sisters and had shown the treatment to Diana, who offered her input. However, the scenes were heavily fictionalised and Diana suggested that he change the inaccuracies. The project never materialised.

Visit our website and discover thousands of
other History Press books.

www.thehistorypress.co.uk